Advance Praise for *Re*

"A brilliant analysis of the current political crises we face at home and abroad and how we might extricate ourselves by returning to our Founding principles. All who value freedom and believe in the American Experiment should read this book."

— Linda Chavez, Fox News analyst
Chairman, Center for Equal Opportunity

"John Agresto cuts through the fog of present-day debates to remind Americans that the way forward in the 21st century must be through a renewed commitment to the nation's founding ideals and institutions. This is a book that will inspire and inform every thoughtful American."

— James Piereson, President
William E. Simon Foundation

"An elegantly written and cogently argued account of how the recovery of America's first principles, rightly understood in the way the Founders themselves understood them, would go a long way toward alleviating the serious problems we face today. ... This book should be required reading for all university students and concerned citizens."

— Edward J. Erler, Senior Fellow
The Claremont Institute

"If you want to understand why we should be patriots, and how to make America lovely and lovable once again, start with this pithy, accessible, instructive book."

— Matthew Franck, Director
William E. and Carol G. Simon Center on
Religion and the Constitution

"Eloquent, lucid, and persuasive ... [Agresto] guides the reader to understand that America stands, first and foremost, for the principle of equality, a principle he then admirably defends from contemporary critics on both the right and the left."

— Ralph A. Rossum
Salvatori Professor of American Constitutionalism
Claremont McKenna College

Books by John Agresto

Mugged by Reality: The Liberation of Iraq and the
Failure of Good Intentions

The Supreme Court and Constitutional Democracy

The Humanist as Citizen:
Essays on the Uses of the Humanities

Tomatoes, Basil, and Olive Oil —
An Italian American Cookbook

Rediscovering America

Liberty, Equality, and the Crisis of Democracy

John Agresto

/-/\/

Asahina and Wallace
Los Angeles
2015
http://www.asahinaandwallace.com

Copyright © 2015 by John Agresto

Published in the United States by Asahina & Wallace, Inc. (http://www.asahinaandwallace.com)

All rights reserved. No part of this publication may be reproduced or transmitted in any form or by any means, electronic or mechanical, including photocopy, recording, digital, or any information strategy and retrieval system now known or to be invented, without permission in writing from the publisher, except by a writer who wishes to quote brief passages in connection with a review or feature written for inclusion in a periodical or broadcast.

ISBN: 978-1-940412-16-0

Library of Congress Control Number: 2015937980

For
Walter Berns and Harry Jaffa

Contents

We find ourselves under the government of a system of political institutions conducing more essentially to the ends of civil and religious liberty than any of which the history of former times tells us. We, when mounting the stage of existence, found ourselves the legal inheritors of these fundamental blessings. We toiled not in the acquirement or establishment of them; they are a legacy bequeathed us by a once hardy, brave, and patriotic, but now lamented and departed, race of ancestors. Theirs was the task (and nobly they performed it) to possess themselves, and through themselves us, of this goodly land, and to uprear upon its hills and its valleys a political edifice of liberty and equal rights; 'tis ours only to transmit these — the former unprofaned by the foot of an invader, the latter undecayed by the lapse of time and untorn by usurpation — to the latest generation that fate shall permit the world to know. This task of gratitude to our fathers, justice to ourselves, duty to posterity, and love for our species in general, all imperatively require us faithfully to perform.

— Abraham Lincoln

"Address before the Young Men's Lyceum of Springfield, Illinois"

January 27, 1838

Preface

I HAVE BEEN, my whole adult life, a student and teacher of politics, history, and the American Constitution. Over these more than 40 years I've seen public interest in the Constitution and the principles of our Founding grow significantly. Yet, at the same time, I've watched the ability of our schools and universities to teach the Constitution and explain our beliefs decline dramatically. It's not that our students have no interest in these ideas. We all know that young American men and women are full of passionate intensity when it comes to matters of equality, justice, freedom, and rights, especially as they think these topics affect them personally. But what's missing is what our nation's deepest and most comprehensive thinkers, our Founders, said and thought about these matters, and what America's best minds might contribute to our awareness and understanding. So our students rely on their teachers, the media, or contemporary opinion to guide them — with the obvious result that all they are taught is whatever is in the air or spouted by their peers, or by celebrities or singers. And little of it is thoughtful.

In order to understand liberty and equality, justice and rights, more clearly and comprehensively, I thought best to take us back to a time when these ideas were first developed, back to when America's Founders wrote our Declaration of Independence and hammered out the Constitution. Because these were then new ideas, revolutionary ideas, our Founders were compelled to defend them, explain them, and think them through with a thoroughness and commitment that has been unrivaled since.

On one level, this is a book written by an old professor for his students, past and future, to help us all better understand the meaning of our principles and the character of our great American experiment.

But I also think that our current political crises — both international upheavals and domestic unrest — have become so overwhelming that only (as the Founders would say) a "recurrence to first principles" will help us all, not simply students but citizens and voters as well, find our way back.

To do so, this book needs to be more than a philosophical or historical review. While I consider myself first and foremost a university administrator and professor, I have never shied away from jumping into politics and policy battles. So, while I might have been tempted to keep this book strictly on a historical, theoretical, or simply academic level, I think I owe it to everyone interested in our common political life and our contemporary problems to speak more broadly as well. If I can make the Founders' thoughts relevant to our life today, or if through them we can work towards viable solutions, I will have accomplished much.

Finally, I have always considered myself as fairly conservative and traditional, and so I intend to direct much of this book not only to Americans in general but to my fellow conservatives in particular. Much has changed in American conservatism over the last half century, not all of it for the better. If I can help conservatives to become not just partisans of the Constitution but knowledgeable of its principles and thoughtful about its philosophy, I will be content.

Despite all my concerns over the future of America's grand experiment in liberal democracy, there is one small but real cause for optimism: With our current crisis of liberty, equality, and government — and no doubt because of it — the American public seems to be all the more ready to think seriously about the meaning of constitutional government, the intent of the Founders, the requirements for proper liberty, and the true nature of our rights. Contrary to an easygoing belief that history is generally progressive and that we surely know more than people dead for almost two centuries, a large swath of the public now thinks that guidance, even wisdom, might be found in the writings of people who wore britches and never heard of a telephone or a car, much less an iPad or a space station.

And, as I hope to show, they are right.

* * * * *

This, then, is a book that will try to explain the core meaning of the Declaration of Independence of 1776 and of the Constitution of 1787. It is a book that rises to defend the intelligence and patriotism of the Founders who wrote those documents and the ideas and the wisdom those documents contain. It is a book centered on a hope: the hope that a renewal in *understanding* the principles of the Founding will lead to a restoration of those principles in our public life, and the hope that such a restoration will mitigate the crisis we are in.

I do not for a moment pretend that this book is an effortless read. The Founders were thoughtful and serious people confronting hard problems. But the temptation to oversimplify is strong. For example, we may think that establishing democratic government is easy — hell, we think that even the most backward and chaotic places should become "democracies." But the Founders didn't think democracy was easy. We may think that rights — our rights to privacy, speech, expression, gun ownership, and a hundred others —

are supreme, perhaps even absolute. But the Founders didn't. We may think that "equality" means taking and giving till our economic and social conditions are roughly the same. But not one of the Founders came close to thinking that. And neither should we.

I hate to have to say this, but making a good and just republic is hard and keeping it even harder. Autocracies are easy; obeying kings, imams, or demagogic leaders is easy. Even simplistic democracies are easy — just accept and obey whatever today's majority desires. But a republic of free men and women requires more than obedience, more even than patriotism. It requires good sense, intelligence, and thoughtfulness on the part of those who rule the country and shape its future — that is, on *our* part.

So I hope in this small book at least to introduce you to the infinite pains the Founders took to be both thoughtful and careful. In it I hope to offer you our Founders' best arguments and highest reasoning. And I hope to make plain so many of the things Americans are working again to understand — checked and balanced government; equality and rights; constitutional democracy; the meaning of liberty, federalism, the place of free enterprise, and the virtues and limits of our ordinary American lives.

I also hope that there's something of value in this book both for those who call themselves liberals as well as those who think of themselves as conservatives.

Let us stay on these contemporary labels — "liberal" and "conservative" — for one moment longer. These days, it often seems that those who like to call themselves "conservative" have the greatest interest in Constitutional matters. But this wasn't always the case, nor should it be the case going forward. People of a certain age can still remember how Sen. Robert

Byrd, a proud New Dealer, would quote passages from his beloved Constitution from memory on the floor of the Senate. Justice Hugo Black — an old fashioned liberal in good standing — was famously devoted to a strict reading of every one of the Constitution's words. While I think this book may speak to contemporary conservatives most directly, all Americans should understand what the Founders accomplished and gave us — what they thought and why they thought it.

The Founders' beliefs were not (as we so blithely say today) merely their "values," nor were they simply rationalizations they used as convenient tools to get their way. I think we will see that their beliefs contained a comprehensive grasp of human nature, human needs, and human desires. We shall see that the Founders' principles go beyond their time and place and have meaning and persuasive power for us today. What they left us was their best effort to understand what liberty and justice might be, and to forge political institutions to reach those goals.

Let me end on a cautionary note. Understanding the thought of the Founders is, in turn, a call for thoughtfulness among ourselves. The Founders shared a set of common principles and ideas — yet they often disagreed, sometimes passionately, about their application. Likewise, when it comes to policy matters, good and honest Americans will also disagree. Should taxes be raised or lowered? Should war be declared or avoided? How can we balance our understanding of individual liberty with the security needs of the country? These and a thousand other issues are helped by understanding principles of the Constitution — but not solved by them.

In giving us a democratic republic governed by certain ideals, the Founders forced us to be a deliberative people. They bequeathed to us principles, ideas, and guidelines, but not always answers. Because of them we are a democratic people who are both blessed and charged with working out our own futures together.

I hope this book can help us do exactly that.

— John Agresto
Santa Fe, New Mexico
January 2015

Acknowledgments

STUDENTS OF AMERICAN POLITICS will think it surpassing strange that I have dedicated this volume to Professors Walter Berns and Harry Jaffa. Walter Berns was my teacher and advisor at Cornell, and everything, *everything* I know about American political thought, the Founders, the place of Liberty in the life of America, and constitutional law begins with him and his classes.

Harry Jaffa I knew because, as a graduate student, I passed along to him a paper I had written on Lincoln as an undergraduate, and he asked me to meet him in California to discuss it. It was an honor to me rarely since matched. Jaffa was and still is America's greatest scholar of Lincoln, of the Declaration of Independence, and of the idea of human equality. There is little in this book that isn't owed to both these great men who died in January of this year, within hours of each other.

But didn't Berns and Jaffa disagree, and disagree ferociously? On the surface, yes; which is why many will think their coming together in this dedication odd. But while they disagreed, I think not at the deepest level. Still, I can only leave it to readers of this book to see if I am true to the ideas of these two scholar-citizens and if, in building on both, I am as persuasive and coherent as they.

The third and most recent godfather of this book is my editor, Robert Asahina. He took what was a narrow academic tract and forced me to broaden its outlook, eschew loquaciousness and opacity (Oh, how he would hate my saying that!), and make it a book that more than only scholars might want to read. In my view, he's America's best editor — thorough, perceptive, and even charitable.

Who else needs to be recognized? The late Werner Dannhauser of Cornell, who was in every way the finest and most charitable of teachers. David Lowenthal of Boston College, who first introduced me to the genius of Abraham Lincoln and was a model of conservative academic gentlemanliness. My colleagues over the years — Bill Shapiro at Oxford College; Bill Bennett; Carol Iannone, editor of *Academic Questions*; Roger Kimball of Encounter Press; Edwin Delattre; Robby George and Brad Wilson of the James Madison Program at Princeton; Josh Mitchell of Georgetown; Eric Brown of the Hudson Institute; Luther Hodges; Linda Chavez; Marc Landy; Ed Erler; David Bolotin; Abe Greenwald of *Commentary* magazine; and Lise Van Boxel, my colleague and friend who first introduced me to Bob Asahina. All of these and dozens of others had some part in the formation of this book, either through their counsel and encouragement or because they didn't hesitate to tell me when they thought I was wrong and why.

Finally, and in so many ways above everyone, my wife of nearly 50 years, Catherine. With never-failing support and dedication, she puts up with it all. For her I have love; for me she has love, plus patience.

Introduction

The Crisis of American Democracy

IT HAS BECOME a commonplace to call the 20th century "The American Century." It was ours, in large measure, because of our economic and military power: We conquered, pacified, and then rebuilt the developed world in all of 50 years following World War II. But it was ours not only because of our power but also because of the force an idea, our idea, our particular *American* idea.

It was a rich and faceted idea. It combined the notion of the equality of all men with the belief in their inherent and inalienable right to be free and independent individuals. It was an idea that worked to break the chains of birth and caste and said that all should be at liberty to pursue whatever their individual talent and work and luck might set before them. In its development and growth it was an idea that struck at titles like *duce*, *fuehrer*, and *commissar* and said that law, by the consent of the governed, should henceforth rule the affairs of men. It was, in sum, the idea set down in our most important and formative document: "that all men are created equal, that they are endowed by their Creator with certain unalienable Rights, that among these are Life, Liberty, and the pursuit of Happiness." So powerful was this notion of a free, equal, and democratic people, that one important commentator towards the end of the last century said that this idea was now permanent and would soon be universal — that we were all present at what he called "the end of history."[1]

Yet who, today, can look at the world and still see liberty and equality in the ascendency? Russia is again rising, with all the oppression and belligerency of the former Soviet Union. In the Middle East, the latest conquests of militant Islamic fundamentalism are erasing even the small scraps of individual rights that were beginning to grow in what were once ancient despotisms. Today, what seems ascendant in too many places is not freedom but tyranny, not equal liberty but equal servitude.

Even more serious is something that we as Americans believed, until just a few short years ago, was unthinkable: that the rise of *democracy itself* would be, in many places around the globe, the harbinger of new and often greater repression. It's not simply the Taliban in Afghanistan or ISIS or al Qaeda in Iraq and Syria that have become the enemy of human liberty. Even our hopes for equal liberty in those countries touched by the democratic reforms of the "Arab Spring" have been dashed. In Russia, Putin may rule both corruptly and with ferocious force, but he does it under the cover and through the mechanism of open elections.

"The desire for freedom," the second President Bush once remarked, "resides in every human heart. ... Over time, and across the Earth, freedom will find a way."[2] There was a time when every American would have said much the same thing. But today that observation seems self-evidently untrue — a hope, a wish, but hardly a statement of fact. Nor did those suppos-

---

[1] Francis Fukuyama, *The End of History and the Last Man* (New York: Free Press, 1992).

[2] George W. Bush, Speech to the U.N. General Assembly, September 21, 2004.

edly yearning to be free see their liberty snatched away from them by would-be tyrants. Time after time, freedom is not rejected by newly minted despots but by *the people themselves,* who increasingly have questions about what we Americans have always seen as our great contribution to human history — the idea of equal liberty.

This growing distrust of liberty became ever more apparent to me starting just over 10 years ago, when I was in Iraq trying to help the Iraqis rebuild their shattered higher educational system as Senior Adviser to the Iraqi Ministry of Higher Education. I arrived not long after Baghdad fell. We were accompanied by many Iraqis who had suffered under the reign of Saddam Hussein. They worked as our assistants, translators, drivers, and advisers. Many, if not most, harbored thoughts of someday coming to America, leaving that ferocious hellhole far behind.

Over the months, however, their image of America began to tarnish, and a few began to change their minds. Not because they no longer saw America as the land of freedom and infinite possibilities, but because they did. With freedom came risks and few guarantees. Some were concerned that they might not get a job, or a good job, in the States. In Iraq, after all, everyone was assured a job, even under Saddam. Some told me they worried that, after coming to America, they might be evicted from their apartment, or fired for no good reason. Stories were everywhere that in America the boss could give your job away to someone else, or the company might go under, or the landlord might think he could get more from other tenants — and they'd all wind up homeless. Yes, many of them had relatives in America who told them that it wasn't anything like that; but they all now had TV, and they all heard the endlessly hyped media stories about the homeless, the unemployed, and the uninsured.

Yes, they knew that in a free country there might be no limit to how far one might rise, or what one's children might accomplish. But there were no assurances either, and many of them had been so cowed by tyranny and enervated by an always-watchful socialist state that they were scared: beaten down and, in a sense, infantilized. Freedom now seemed not exhilarating but frightening.

If the first concern the Iraqis had about freedom was the uncertainty of it, the second and far more serious problem was what they saw as freedom's destructive side — especially its seemingly corrosive effect on religion, on morality, and on the family. This was a much deeper problem, one that couldn't be deflected by any talk of social-welfare projects and safety nets. I remember one earnest young man from the State Department telling a group of tribal leaders that, yes, Americans enjoyed extensive freedom of religion. In the U.S., a person could practice his religion without fear of persecution. As far as I could tell, this seemed to everyone assembled a reasonably good thing. The young man then added that not only would no one be persecuted for his beliefs, but religious people of every creed lived peacefully and equally with one another, even with people who chose not to believe in God at all. With that, you could see the thought come across every face: "Why is this so good? Why would anyone be proud of a place where ignoring God is something people praise?" Finally someone asked what amounted to this: "Could a person in America be free to speak against God, or curse God?" To which the awkward response was, "Well, yes. I mean, in America we have freedom of speech as well as of religion, so, er, while I'm not saying that would be a good thing…" The answer was, of course, true, and for any number of important reasons we Americans would not change it. But to the assembled believers, what we see as central and vital freedoms seemed impious, wicked, and dangerous.

There were, to be sure, even more awkward things about American liberty that my Iraqi friends had never heard of. I'm certain they did not know that a few years before, public funds in America were used to subsidize the showing, as "art," of a crucifix immersed in a jar of urine. When Christian groups protested, they were met with jeers from those lawyerly and sophisticated Americans who proclaimed that freedom of expression and artistic rights could not be trammeled. Christians in Iraq were few, but even non-Christians might feel that if this was what Americans thought of as "freedom," they'd just as soon forgo the pleasure. Nor could they have seen a future time when our State Department would denounce, as a flagrant violation of political rights and free expression, the imprisonment of a group of Russian women who styled themselves a "pussy riot" after having desecrated the sanctuary of St. Savior's Cathedral in Moscow. Was this what America's great defense of "rights" had degenerated to — defending the desecration of churches?[3]

But the discomfort I saw among so many in the Middle East went beyond the way liberty seemed to undermine traditional religious notions. I was present, in 2004, for the revelations in Iraq about the abuses at the prison at Abu Ghraib. As reported in the press, Abu Ghraib was the locus of American coercion

---

[3] Lest we get the impression that it is only in Muslim countries where the tide against freedom is rising, consider all we see these days in Russia, as well as other associated nations in the former Soviet bloc. Note again that this rejection of the latest versions of liberty and individual rights, while surely instigated by Mr. Putin, does seem to have wide and deep *popular* support.

and torture. But that wasn't exactly how the Iraqis viewed it. Torture, as every Iraqi knew, sometimes firsthand, was done with acid, amputations, red-hot metal, or electric drills to the back. Here, instead of torture and physical pain, Iraqis saw debasement — sexual humiliation, not disfigurement. Iraqi men were forced onto other men while American soldiers, including women, watched. Iraqis were made to strip naked and walk on all fours like dogs, with a smiling woman reservist holding the leash. Iraqi prisoners were raped by other men, or forced to watch while a female American soldier had sex with her paramour. In the end, what my Iraqi friends saw was the joy the Americans seemed to display at degrading not only Iraqis, but themselves as well. This was moral, not physical, degeneracy — disfigurement not of the body but of the soul.

Is this what they do in the land of the free? Those of us who were in Iraq at the time tried to portray the happenings at Abu Ghraib as an aberration. But the Iraqis saw it as something cultural, something that grew naturally out of a society that had now "liberated" itself from all the shackles of conventional morality. To those I met abroad there was — and will be for many years — nothing more important than religion, honor, and family. And it seemed that it was exactly those things that contemporary America has set in its sights to flatten.

Let me be as blunt as I can: To much of the world, America seems to have reached a point today where there is no longer a line separating rights from desires, or liberty from what used to be called licentiousness. Indeed, many of our fellow citizens agree that any attempt to draw such a line must stem from either nasty prejudice or religious hokum. Even within the Republican Party, the partisans of traditional morality, of "family values," seem to be losing ground every day to a surging libertarian wing, a faction whose policies on drug use, unfettered freedom of expression, and sometimes abortion seem indistinguishable from those on the left. How many of the old political and social constraints on what used to be viewed as wrong or immoral behavior are now gone, in the name of personal freedom and various "rights"? Of those that still exist, how many are ridiculed all across the nation, particularly on the coasts?

We talk endlessly about how we have to understand others in this more multicultural age. But we seem blind to the most important things that make other cultures "other." So we act in ways they find perplexing at best and shameful at worse, then wonder why the seeds of democratic liberty we have tried to plant abroad seem not to take root. We have viewed every desire a potential "right"; weakened conventional social order in the name of self-expression and freedom; set aside older views of obligation, self-restraint, responsibility, decency, and morality; and condemned as religious prejudice any preference for traditional family arrangements. And having done all this, we've made freedom the father of what the vast majority of the world understands to be ignoble and immoral.

To the world, what was once a most beautiful thing, the American promise of liberty, now seems to have lost much of her loveliness.[4]

It would be wrong to leave you with the impression that the problem with our postmodern understanding of liberty is primarily an issue of foreign policy or a problem of how others view America from abroad. These new understandings of liberty have had at least

---

[4] This echo of Irving Kristol famed essay, "'When Virtue Loses All Her Loveliness' – Some Reflections on Capitalism and 'the Free Society'" (*The Public Interest*, No. 21, Fall 1970), is not accidental.

two deleterious effects on our country domestically, too.

First, the development of new "rights" — usually rights imposed judicially or developed in bureaucratic offices — has undermined what have long been thought to be the most basic rights of a free society. Can a family business conduct its affairs with deference to its religious beliefs, or even its philosophical beliefs, or must it bend its practices to the demands of others claiming newer rights? Will religious groups be able to *believe* whatever they choose, but not *act* on their faith? How many will be shamed into silence for fear of losing their jobs, or be accused of bias, prejudice, or even hatred, for expressing what were, until yesterday, ordinary opinions and traditional views?

Let's turn from the public square to the halls of academia. I've been a professor long enough to know that there is more freedom of discussion around any random family dinner table than there is on most university campuses. What were once America's foundational freedoms — religion, property, speech, deliberation — have all been truncated in university settings under enforced "sensitivity" and the latest versions of contemporary "rights."

But the problem goes further. Liberty, it is true, has always had a worrisome side. Left free, speech could be fraudulent, libelous, obscene. The rightful pursuit of property could sometimes become mere selfishness, rapaciousness, greed. Laws, of course, could rectify the worst abuses of liberty. But a decent society always relied on a few things more. Let's call them "conservative" things: traditional moral teachings, religion, admonitions to self-restraint, and long-respected historical conventions. These, often more than laws, had the potential to keep liberty from degenerating into license.[5] But it is exactly these things — religion, convention, tradition, morality — that are now seen not as moderating our selfish demands and helping to make our liberty civil, but as the enemies of liberty itself.

Finally, since these new rights are, as I said, most often imposed judicially or proclaimed by administrative fiat, what is lost is perhaps the most central and inestimable right that any free society can have: the right of the people to govern themselves.

* * * * *

If we turn our attention from the problem with rights and liberty and look at the second major principle of the American Idea — equality — we see what in many ways is an even greater crisis.

Americans have known, at least since the time that Alexis de Tocqueville wrote *Democracy in America,* that the principle of equality could be both an ally of human liberty and its greatest enemy. "I think that democratic communities have a natural taste for freedom," Tocqueville wrote. "Left to themselves, they will seek it, cherish it, and view any privation of it with regret. But for equality, their passion is ardent, insatiable, incessant, invincible: they call for equality in freedom; and if they cannot obtain that, they still call for equality in slavery."[6]

To be certain, "equal rights," "equal opportunity," and "equality under law" all bespeak the intimate connection that equality properly understood has with liberty. But how could giving preferences on the basis of race or color possibly pass for the equal protection of the laws? Or, to point to an issue that has so re-

---

[5] "License": Even the word seems now antique; a word reserved for dogmatists and grandparents.

[6] Alexis de Tocqueville, *Democracy in America,* Volume 2, part II, chapter 1.

cently burst onto the political scene, when did fairness
and justice move from equal rights and equal opportunity to a demand for greater equality of income and
greater equality of wealth? What changed in the
American political mind that it could go from trying to
give all the equal chance to be everything that they
might be — with the natural result that some would
rise higher and others fall short — to the highly problematic and, dare I say, unjust and illiberal view that
real differences of wealth, rank, and respect are inher-
ently unfair?

How could the right to express opinions on social,
cultural, familial, or political issues be stigmatized as
"hate speech" because of the mere suggestion that not
all lifestyle choices might be equally worthy? How did
it happen that all cultures are now proclaimed to be
equal, no way of life superior, no habits inferior, no
books "great," and no writer, thinker, poet, or civilization ever allowed to be praised or acclaimed or, as is
said so disdainfully today, "privileged"? Is all this
what the once dignified principle of equality really
means?

* * * * *

Where do we start? How do we begin once more to
see that liberty is not at war with morality and right;
that individual freedoms can and must subsist with
national security, domestic tranquility, and a concern
for the general welfare, and that liberty and equality
need not be enemies but allies in the pursuit of human
happiness?

One place to begin is by rejecting the temptation to
turn the richness and comprehensiveness of the
Founders' vision into today's simplistic and ideological slogans. Look, for example, at some of our current
formulations. Take equality: Didn't Jefferson say that

all men are created equal? Yes. And isn't it obvious that today, after well over 200 years, people still aren't "equal" in all their possessions? Yes, it's true. So why do we not fight harder (the ideologue says) for greater redistribution of wealth, or for the equalization of power internationally, or for increased central planning to guarantee a more egalitarian distribution of goods?

Or consider the ideas of democracy and liberty. Are we a democracy? Fundamentally, yes. And democracy means rule by the people, right? Again, yes. So therefore (the urge to simplify says) those things that slow down or stop majority rule should be unconstitutional, right? Well, maybe not. Or, consider a common over-simplification from the other side: Weren't the Founders in favor of protecting minority rights? Yes. Weren't they also against the "tyranny of the majority"? Yes. So therefore isn't it unconstitutional to push policies that restrict what minorities see as their "rights"? Well, no, not always; sometimes not at all. While the Founders were against tyranny of the majority, they were against tyranny of the *minority* just as much.

Such questions point to one of the most important issues the Founders faced: the problem of combining liberty with popular rule, or making freedom compatible with democracy. But to do this required a comprehensive understanding of human nature, of the demands of freedom, of the rights of both individuals and the public — and skill, unprecedented prudential *skill*. It could never have been done by simply digging into a grab bag of platitudes, clichés, and slogans.

Today, this may be one of the hardest things to comprehend: that the Founders didn't live by slogans. They wanted to establish a country that was both democratic and also respectful of legitimate individual rights. They believed in the fundamental equality of all human beings, but they didn't offer that insight as a warrant to promote universal sameness, or to restrict human rights, or to equalize property, or to pull down the fine or the beautiful or the successful or the cultured. They wanted a country that would combine liberty with domestic tranquility, equality with support for the extraordinary, popular rule with justice. Their goal was to make a government strong enough to defend us, efficient and competent enough to assist us, yet restrained enough to keep from oppressing us. None of this would be accomplished by spouting slogans.

So how is it that, despite our rediscovered desire to live in the light of the Founders' principles, such complex and serious issues have become so dumbed down, on both the right and the left? How is it that, our political discourse has, in the last half century, become ever more impoverished and turned so far from common sense?

If the problem is that what was once rich and complex has become simplified and easy, I would suggest that the first place to look is to that great modern simplifier: the media. Although politically interested Americans are taking renewed interest in the Constitution, they're not learning much of substance from the daily papers or TV. The public is to be forgiven if it assumes that the Founding Fathers spoke in sound bites and wrote a Constitution made up of catch-phrases and tag lines. People are certainly not being helped to understand the ideas behind what the Founders accomplished. Ideas are hard to grasp, and the easy way to make something fit between commercial breaks is to simplify, simplify, simplify.

Moreover, as the media know, the best way to keep peoples' attention is not only to simplify ideas but to radicalize them. It surely makes for more exciting television. So if the Founders were concerned about all types of concentrated power, which they were, simplify the notion, then call on spokesmen who will radicalize it: "Smash the corporate structure" and "occupy Wall Street" on the left, or flirt with shutting down the government on the right. (After all, if government is almost always "the problem," why not shut it down?) The media often take what could have been a true debate — an informed and informative debate — and turn it into a clash of dogmatic stances and a parade of slogans.

Nor have our schools and universities added to the general public's understanding of our Constitution. Yes, some conscientious civics teacher might still make her class memorize the Constitution's Preamble. And the Bill of Rights is the ground of a number of college courses on contemporary politics, as well as the occasion for endless (and usually maddeningly vapid) late-night dorm bull sessions. Nonetheless, the ideas contained in the American Constitution and the thought and reasons of the Founders are not something the schools or our universities seem to find all that important or enlightening.

In fact, our Founding documents and the thought of the Founders might find themselves treated more shabbily in our schools and colleges than even in the media! Why? Simply put, while the media often simplify or radicalize the ideas of the Founders, our schools and universities have a perverse habit of dismissing them. Given all we now know (as students are often taught), how could a document penned before all the important revolutions of the last two centuries — in industry, communications, gender relations, health care, warfare, intelligence gathering, not to mention our "modern" understanding of democracy, equality, and morality itself — still be relevant?

In this view, the Founders' ideas are simply out of date. But there's another and more insidious way to dismiss them, and it's a way all our students hear from their earliest history lessons through their courses in college: The Founders were rich white men who had slaves. And why would *anyone* pay serious attention to self-interested plutocrats and nasty racists? Or, in the recent words of a prominent law professor, why should anyone revere an "archaic, idiosyncratic and downright evil" document?[7]

Of course professors with such opinions can be dismissed as cloistered academics out of touch with the real world. But professors often write textbooks — and not simply the high-priced tomes they peddle in their own classes but books that get adopted in our grade schools and high schools.[8] From there, what might have seemed simply academic balderdash gets peddled to the young as gospel.

The other direction these "academic" teachings move is not only downward to the schools and the young but upwards to our elites and our policy makers. Indeed, so disparaging can some elite Americans be of the views of the Founders that even a sitting Supreme Court justice can go abroad, to a nation that

---

[7] Louis Michael Seidman, "Let's Give Up On the Constitution," *The New York Times,* December 31, 2012. Professor Seidman teaches Constitutional law at Georgetown University.

[8] Consider the late but still omnipresent Howard Zinn: "The Founding Fathers did lead the war for independence from Britain. But they did not do it for the equal right of all to life, liberty, and equality. Their intention was to set up a new government that would protect the property of slave owners, land speculators, merchants, and bondholders" (*The Progressive,* October 2001). Professor Zinn's best known work, *A People's History of The United States* (New York: Harper-Collins, 1980), is built around that thesis and, in addition to being one of the most meretricious books ever penned, is also perhaps the one most assigned in school history classes.

seemed at the time to have some interest in understanding liberty and establishing democratic forms, and tell them not to look at the American Constitution but to look elsewhere![9] How shameful; how unbelievably sad.

So now, knowing full well the forces arrayed against us — the media, the schools, and so many of our intellectual and political elites — let us try again to understand the Founders and their vision, and begin anew the task of reconstituting our Republic.

---

[9] This was Justice Ruth Ginsburg telling an Egyptian audience that if they wanted to have a truly free country, "I would not look to the U.S. Constitution if I were drafting a constitution in the year 2012." Indeed, if they wanted to see "a great piece of work," they should look at something like the constitution of South Africa (Ruth Bader Ginsburg, interview with Al-Hayat TV, February 1, 2012).

'All Men Are Created Equal'

I. One night, a member of the White House staff found President Lincoln polishing his boots. "Mr. President, you blacken our own boots!?!" To which the President responded, "Well, whose boots do you think I blacken?"

II. A bank in Indiana was looking for a teller, and a young man from back East applied for the job. The bank needed a letter of recommendation, so the young man had a close family friend write for him.

"The young man you see before you," the letter read, "comes from a long line of the most distinguished citizens of Massachusetts. His great grandfather was a Winthrop, one of the greatest and most pious preachers in America. His mother is a Lowell, and his father is a member of the Cabot family, both sides containing leaders of industry, eminent statesmen, and the most renowned philanthropists in the Commonwealth. I'm sure you will find their offspring to be excellent in every way."

To this the president of the bank wrote back: "I fear there's been a dreadful mistake. We were considering the young man for the post of bank teller. We were not planning on using him for breeding purposes."

* * * * *

"We hold these truths to be self evident — That all men are created equal, that they are en-

dowed by their Creator with certain unalienable Rights. ..."

— The Declaration of Independence

* * * * *

"WE HOLD THESE TRUTHS to be self-evident — That
all men are created equal": In 1776, Thomas Jefferson
wrote these words near the very beginning of our Declaration of Independence. With these few simple
words, America began its revolution against the British crown, and we were launched on the road to national independence. These words helped form us into
the greatest and most lasting democracy in the modern world. It was these words that Abraham Lincoln
relied on in freeing the slaves, and these words that
gave life to all the varied civil rights movements that
have taken place in America over the last 200 years. It
is fair to say that these words are the most important
political words ever written in our country. Politically,
socially, and even morally, everything we are stems
from these few words.

Still, while known to every school child and repeated in millions of public documents and patriotic
speeches, the words still seem a stumbling block, even
an embarrassment, to partisans on both the left and
right.

Where, the left might point out, are these words
applied in this country? In our inner cities and slums?
In our race relations? In our economic life, where
some earn billions each year and others subsist on
food stamps? When were these words ever true?
When there was slavery? Or under Jim Crow? Or
when women couldn't vote? The words of the Declaration are not false in theory. But, the left points out,
they surely appear false in fact. So the only appropriate goal of politics and policy is to make these lofty

words finally come true. At the heart of contemporary American liberalism is the aim of making America hold to its promise and become a place where all people are treated as Jefferson said they deserve — equally.

Conservatives in America often read those same words in the Declaration and they also worry, but for different reasons. What concerns the right is that the idea of equality gets interpreted not as equality of rights, or equality of opportunity, or equality before the law, but as equality literally. What worries many conservatives is that so many of today's liberal politicians and social engineers believe that equality means the redistribution of wealth, the relativizing of all lifestyles and desires, the destruction of rights in the name of equal treatment, and a general leveling of economic, social, and cultural life. When conservatives hear the contemporary cognates of equality — "fairness," "social justice," and "redistribution" — they fear that what is afoot is little more than envy masquerading as right, or some new variant of socialism thinking itself to be justice. And the right probably secretly wishes that Jefferson had been clearer and less flowery. Instead of mentioning "equality" he should have talked only about what follows in the Declaration — independence, rights, liberty, and honor.

As I hope to show, both sides — especially the more radical elements of each side — are wrong when they see Jefferson's "equality" as code for leveling or redistribution. To the right it must be said that equality is actually a conservative principle of the highest order. Properly understood, equality is the very foundation of our rights and the principle that has made our American life distinctive, even "exceptional." And American liberals, insofar as they think that "created equal" isn't enough — that men and women should now be *made* "equal" in all the most important aspects of life — are flirting with a doctrine that is both wrong and dangerous.

I do believe that, despite their various policy differences, both liberals and conservatives, when they find themselves attached to simpler notions of equality — for example, to the idea of equal opportunity, or equality of rights, or equal treatment under law — are indeed children of the Declaration and heirs to all the good that comes from this manifest and self-evident truth that "all men are created equal."

However, the center has a hard time holding these days. And, as more extreme notions of equality arise, the more ideologues and demagogues jump into the fight, and the worse America becomes.

How Today's Liberalism Distorts the Declaration

Since the idea of human equality is fundamental to our national self-understanding, we need to have as clear a picture as possible as to what that might mean.

The battle between rich and poor seems coeval with all of human social and political life. Solving this problem was of central concern to all those important democratic theorists who helped shape the thinking of our Founders. So it should not surprise us that philosophers and social scientists as well as politicians and citizens continue to debate the matter today.

Among liberals, Thomas Piketty is the most serious of the current political economists in the fight for income equality and economic redistribution.[10] Piketty takes almost infinite pains to prove what most people might find commonplace: that ordinary people who

---

[10] Thomas Piketty, *Capital in the Twenty-First Century* (Cambridge: Belknap Press of Harvard University, 2014).

live off their incomes will virtually never do as well as people who can invest and live off the return on their capital. Building on this near-obvious truth, Piketty predicts that, since the rate of return on capital will almost always exceed the rate of growth in the economy, in the long run wealth will be concentrated in the hands of a small plutocracy, in investors who amass immense fortunes from the returns on their capital assets.

Piketty makes two key arguments about economic inequality: First, that the gap between the extremely wealthy on one side and virtually everyone else on the other will grow ever larger, and second, that those at the top will be not only few but permanent, and able to amass immense social and political power. Because of this widening and permanent disparity of wealth, democracies risk "significant political upheaval" from the backlash of the many who are left behind against the inordinate political influence of the super-wealthy minority.

Some parts of Piketty's analysis have appeal across the political spectrum: his observations on how unearned and permanent wealth breaks the link that market economies have historically forged between work and reward, and his attacks on "crony capitalism" and worries about globalization could have come straight from a Tea Party pamphlet. But both his general analysis and his policy prescriptions (a global progressive tax not on income but on wealth, for example) also speak directly to today's liberal egalitarians longing for an academic voice to support their ideological leanings.

Yet Piketty's description of permanent wealth accumulation in only a few families seems wrong as history and unlikely as prediction. Today's billionaires are no longer named Rockefeller, Harriman, Carnegie, or Hill, for example, but Gabbana and Jobs and Dos Santos — people whose rise overtook others and who will, in their turn, be themselves overtaken. And why should the civic body find these fortunes so unjust or so destructive of democratic life that a massive confiscation of estates is necessary to save democracy from internal revolution? Where — except on the fringes of the activist left or in the speeches of demagogues — are the masses of dissatisfied citizens clamoring for confiscatory redistribution? Curiously, the wealthy, even the "obscenely wealthy," are rarely the objects of hatred, though they might be the objects of envy. In fact, the super-rich often find themselves admired for their success and praised for their philanthropy. There have been no massive protests that Oprah Winfrey or Warren Buffett is buying our elections, or that Bill Gates just has too much money.[11]

In fact, the only people who seem truly to be riled up about the phenomenon are not the masses but liberal — and usually well-off — elites. While much of Piketty's analysis supports the left's view that economic inequality is wide and deep and increasing worldwide, his predictions of doom are not very persuasive. And Piketty's remedies — for instance, a global and confiscatory wealth tax administered through some international body — are so politically implausible that not much energy will or should be expended on them.

So why has Piketty's work become such a touchstone, when its predictions are unlikely and its policy

---

[11] To be sure, there are charges that the Koch brothers and other similar "plutocrats" control America's elections. But for every Koch on one side there always seems to be a Soros or Steyer on the other, each with wads of cash. Then again, there are surely those on the right who think that "the media" control elections just as the left frets over the power of wealthy donors. (With the difference, of course, that the right never seems to call for the nationalization of big media wealth.)

prescriptions are unrealistic? For the left, the problem with income inequality often lies less in its results than in its manifest injustice, its essential "unfairness." As former President Clinton recently framed it, the problem is not so much the consequences of income inequality but the "moral outrage" of the "inequality problem" itself.[12] It is this belief that inequality is immoral *in essence* that today most separates a large part of the progressive left from the conservative right.

Let's look at President Obama's oft-repeated statements on the economy, for example: The good thing about political action and community organizing is that, through them, one can help bring about "redistributive change."[13] The wealthy, we are told, have been allowed to avoid paying "their fair share."[14] What is needed is more ways to "spread the wealth"[15] and redistribute "unneeded" income.[16] The enemies of greater economic equality in America are "millionaires and billionaires."[17] Not only in his 2014 State of the Union address but more comprehensively a few weeks before, the president underscored it all by singling out the core of the problem: The issue is "income inequality."[18]

---

[12] These were Clinton's remarks at the inauguration of New York City Mayor Bill de Blasio, whose campaign for that office was based squarely upon the notion of the injustice of income and power inequality.

[13] Speech at Loyola University, October 19, 1998; WEBZ radio interview, October 26, 2001. It was in this same interview that Sen. Obama criticized the Civil Rights movement for not having devoted enough energy to this same "redistributive change."

[14] Third Presidential Debate, October 22, 2012; State of the Union Address, January 24, 2013, and elsewhere.

[15] From the infamous dialogue with "Joe the Plumber," October 13, 2008.

[16] Press conference, July 11, 2011.

[17] Rose Garden speech, September 18, 2001.

[18] Address to the Center for American Progress, December 4, 2013.

There is, the president pointed out, "a dangerous and growing inequality" in this country. Indeed, contrary to the equality proclaimed by Jefferson, America is a nation that today has become "profoundly unequal." So pervasive is this crisis of inequality that all Americans understand it, and increasingly have "the bad taste that the system is rigged."

This is, of course, a massive indictment of America, framed in seemingly the most American of terms: Yes, the president was saying, the idea of the Declaration is true: All people are indeed to be treated as equal. But, under this indictment, while that might be true in theory, nothing could be further from the truth in fact.

It was for this purpose and perhaps this one alone that the president declared that his presidency would be a "transformational" event.[19] Like the presidents before him whom he often cites and who also used the notion of equality to change the course of our history — Lincoln, FDR, and Lyndon Johnson — this president would make the issue of economic inequity in America central to his presidency. The hope was that under his leadership, as under theirs, what the left understands as the *promise* of equality in America would come closer to being the *fact* of equality in America.

Although conservatives tend to see the president as extreme when it comes to matters of economic redistribution, there are others who actually go further.

For example, consider Sen. Elizabeth Warren: "There is nobody in this country who got rich on his own. Nobody," she declared pointing out that the rich

---

[19] October 2008, in a campaign visit to Columbia, Missouri: "Now, I just have two words for you tonight: five days. Five days. After decades of broken politics in Washington, and eight years of failed policies from George W. Bush, and 21 months of a campaign that's taken us from the rocky coast of Maine to the sunshine of California, we are five days away from fundamentally transforming the United States of America."

can only get rich thanks to a "social contract" that provides a decent, functioning society in which they can prosper. "I want to be clear," she lectured the business community. "You moved your goods to market on the roads the rest of us paid for. You hired workers the rest of us paid to educate. You were safe in your factory because of police forces and fire forces that the rest of us paid for. ... Part of the underlying social contract is you take a hunk of that and pay it forward for the next kid who comes along."[20]

To conservatives, this seems to turn Jefferson's Declaration squarely on its head. A notion of equality that once highlighted our independence from unwarranted coercive power now has become twisted to underscore our subordination to the collective. No longer does it seem that freedom lives symbiotically with equality; now it looks as if what we are and all we make and own can be held at the pleasure of the "social contract." That is, contrary to the Declaration, our rights are now controlled by the very government we established "to secure our rights"! How is this different from saying, "You owe your lives and possessions to the grace and favor of the Crown, since it's his roads you travel on and his lands you live on"? Isn't a sentiment like that radically contrary to what Mr. Jefferson was saying?

Of course, insofar as the ability to rise socially or economically is *cut off* in America — if equal *opportunity* is stymied by Jim Crow laws or by policies that mandate unreasonable preferences to certain groups or disable people from competing fairly and equally because of race or gender or qualities unrelated to merit or ability — then the system is indeed unfair. Or where certain individuals or businesses or corpora-

---

[20] Speech at Andover, Massachusetts, August 2011, and elsewhere.

tions or unions collude with those in power to maintain their income and privileges — "crony capitalism," as it is often called — then again the system is unfair. Where economic inequality is permanent, where the rich are protected from falling and the poor are prevented from rising, there the system is not only unequal but unfair and unjust. On these points liberals and conservatives should agree.

There was also a time when those on the left could demand a redistribution of wealth because those who had great wealth got it nefariously: monopolists, robber barons, Ponzi scheme operators, currency manipulators, financiers who rigged the markets with friends in power, exploiters of various stripes. Again, I think both left and right would agree that such activities distort the market economy in ways that are criminal and corrupt.

If the concern were simply bringing thieves, manipulators, and monopolists to justice, there would be little to distinguish the left today from moderate liberals, or Teddy Roosevelt, or even Tea Party conservatives who have been among the loudest in railing against bailouts for special-interest groups and favored treatment for financiers and Wall Street bankers. If the cause of poverty or even stagnant mobility were the direct result of laws or policies that directly stifle equal opportunity, then redress in some form or other would have widespread support across the political spectrum.

But those concerns are not exactly the issue in the president's lament that so many have so much more than others, or the senator's belief that men and women don't actually own what they worked hard to build. To see the grounds of those arguments, let us here turn from academic economic analyses and political speechifying to contemporary political philosophy.

To say that increased equality is needed not to compensate those who were stolen from, or even to increase economic opportunity for all, but that inequalities are *in themselves* unjust is a philosophical and ideological conclusion. And it's one not hard to trace. As with so many radical notions, these views began not in the streets and barrios of the poor or on the factory floor, but in the universities.

In virtually every American university, John Rawls's belief in "justice as fairness" holds sway today as the last word in moral and political theory.[21] Rawls's *A Theory of Justice* is unquestionably the most influential book on the subject in the last 100 years — a book that the young Barack Obama no doubt read and appreciated at Occidental and Columbia. Rawls argues that justice lies in rewarding people not on the basis of their merit or success or work, or even their productivity, but rather simply on the basis of "fairness."[22] Justice does not consist in letting people enjoy the unequal fruits of their labor (or their parents' labor) or any other benefit that they accrued by reason of their unequal labor or talent or education or intelligence or even luck — qualities distributed unequally and unmerited at birth.[23] Rather, true justice "nullifies the accidents of natural endowment," resulting in a system where "income and wealth are evenly shared."[24] Thus, to Rawls, a just society is not

---

[21] John Rawls, *A Theory of Justice* (Cambridge: Harvard University Press, 1971).

[22] Ibid., p.11, sec. 3, and throughout.

[23] To "permit the distribution of wealth and income to be determined by the natural distribution of abilities and talents" is an outcome which "is arbitrary from a moral perspective," pp. 73-4, sec. 13.

[24] Ibid., p. 15, sec 3, and p. 62, sec 11. Any deviation from this simple equality of wealth and income is only moral if the resulting difference can in fact be proven to be to "everyone's" advantage, "and at the same time," p. 61, sec. 11.

one that encourages each person to be all that he or she might hope to be, nor even one that rewards its citizens on the basis of their work or talent or the results of their labor. Rather justice is "fairness" in the "determin[ation of] social benefits" and the proper and more equal distribution of goods already produced.[25]

For this reason, the president can support policies that penalize the rich even if they have only minimal impact in raising the condition of the poor. "Well, Charlie," as Mr. Obama explained to TV commentator Charles Gibson, "what I've said is I would look at raising the capital gains tax for purposes of fairness."[26] Not to raise taxes to lower the deficit, or to fund increases in scientific research, or to increases the nation's defenses, or even to devote more funds to education or poverty programs. No, simply "for purposes of fairness."[27] Does raising the minimum wage or demanding increases in overtime pay help the poor? Yes, it aids some, though it most assuredly hurts others, even among the poor. But what it does do is redistribute money and lower the unequal possession of wealth, cutting into the "unmerited" profits of businesses. After all, justice should demand that we understand (in the president's words) when people have "made enough money."[28] To use an old metaphor, bringing down the mountains and hills is good in itself, even if it doesn't do all that much for the valleys.

According to this logic, if policies are in themselves "just," they are worth the costs of decreased produc-

---

[25] Ibid., p.11, sec 3, et passim.

[26] April 17, 2008.

[27] Again, "justice," in this view, consists less in the maximization of prosperity than in its proper distribution, in "fairness." Indeed, "there is no reason to think that just institutions will maximize the good." Rawls, op. cit., p. 30, sec. 6.

[28] Speech in Quincy, Illinois, April 28, 2010.

tivity and lower general prosperity. Is it not morally right for *all* to have health insurance even if the cost of policies rise, access to doctors becomes harder, and the general quality of care falls? After all, who ever promised that justice would be easy or increased equality be without its costs?

These policy examples show how our contemporary and more radical idea of equality affects our domestic political life. But why should it stop at the water's edge? After all, doesn't the Declaration proclaim the equality of *all* men? Why should America, with comparatively small a population, be allowed to consume as much as it does? Why should any American be proud of a country filled with abundance and everyday enjoyments while others live not only in want but often in misery? Doesn't justice demand that in fairness we share our blessings with all? America is to the world as the "obscenely wealthy" are to the rest of us in this country. And if, "for purposes of fairness," our homegrown rich should be taken down a peg or two, how much more should America itself be taken down for its "consumerism" or "materialism" or carbon footprint – or even simply its prosperity and good fortune -- in the face of poverty and misery worldwide?

And if the flattening of *economic* inequalities both domestically and internationally is part of the idea of human equality, why not the leveling of other goods, too — for instance, the leveling of power? This is no longer a radical thought. No nation, as the president intimated, should consider itself "exceptional" or superior to others. Does not the equality of all people require the supplanting of "national interest" as the guide to foreign policy and its replacement by the egalitarian belief that no nation should exercise power over others? "I pledge to you," President Obama said to the Summit of the Americas in 2009, "that we seek an equal partnership," a partnership in which "there is no senior partner and no junior partner."[29] In Egypt later that year, the president pointed to our Declaration of Independence and declared that the "ideal" that "all are created equal" should have meaning not only "within our borders," but also "around the world." No longer should there be "any world order that elevates one nation or group of people over another."[30]

Thus, as much of left currently understands it, equality is *without doubt* the most radical, most "transformational" of all ideas. No wonder conservatives are concerned!

How Conservatives Misunderstand the Declaration

Let's return again to the words of the Declaration of Independence: "We hold these truths to be self evident — That all men are created equal, that they are endowed by their Creator with certain unalienable rights. ...."

I think it fair to say that, while liberals have difficulty with *the fact* of the Declaration's proclamation that all men are created equal, conservatives seem to have an equally deep problem, a worry about *the truth* of those words. To put it bluntly: To some conservatives, the words seem wrong, theoretically false, and dangerous.

Conservatives like the idea of rights, of individual liberty. But the idea of "equality" smacks too much of

---

[29] Address to the Summit of the Americas opening ceremony, Hyatt Regency, Port of Spain, Trinidad and Tobago, April 17, 2009.

[30] Speech in Cairo, Egypt, June 4, 2009. Carried to its full conclusion, would not egalitarian "fairness" demand that all nations have not only equal respect but also equal power, equal standing, equal weaponry? This notion of finally making all "nations" and "groups" equal simply underscores the genuine danger of the left's radicalization of Jefferson's self-evident truth.

socialism, of the radical redistribution of wealth, of the nanny state with its dependent citizens all thinking they're entitled to what others worked hard to earn. Why, they might ask, did Jefferson have to muddy the waters by combining rights, which are good, with equality, which is a pernicious idea and often the enemy of rights?

But Jefferson was hardly a thoughtless person, nor were the patriots of the Revolution who signed on to this Declaration a glib or careless bunch. When they said that human equality was not only true but "self evidently" true, it wasn't just rhetoric. They meant it exactly that way — that in some important and fundamental way, we are all equal to each other. So much so that our inalienable rights and our nation's independence both seem to hinge on this truth.

Although the two small tales that head up this chapter — the one involving Lincoln's boots and the one about the bank teller — are surely invented, they express a sentiment we, as Americans, all share. I've lived in a number of countries where subjects would think it perfectly natural that a president would command others to polish his shoes, countries where it's simply expected that ancestry and connections give a person an advantage against others. But America is different, even radically different, from the vast majority of other places not only in history but also today. America is exceptional in part because we have a deep, quiet, unassuming belief that "all men are created equal" — even the sons of aristocrats and the daughters of day laborers. In America, even young children are imbued with a sense of equality: "You're not better than I am" is a common childhood retort, even when the person to whom it is aimed actually *is* better. Families in America have likewise become more and more egalitarian. Gone are the days when a father would will all his property to his firstborn son and leave the rest to fend for themselves. And it would be morally unthinkable for parents to feed, clothe, and protect one child better than another.

Yet, while we Americans have both a deep-seated sense of egalitarianism, we still find the words of our Declaration perplexing. Even though the words are stirring, touching chords of sentiment within us, what exactly do they mean? How and in what ways are we equal? We see inequality around us all the time — differences in wealth, in talent, in ability, in health, in social status, in power, in influence, in rights, in education, even in the esteem of our neighbors. So what in the world could "created equal" mean? Since it cannot mean that we actually *are* equal, does it imply that the government should use its power to *make* us more equal? If so, what should all of us be equal *in*? Should *all* inequalities be eliminated, including inequalities of talent, intelligence, ambition, beauty, social standing, and influence over others?

* * * * *

There is, of course, a long history of attacks on the meaning of the Declaration from the right — especially that part of the right that once defended slavery and segregation. That group looks at Jefferson's words as nonsense, false, perhaps even (as one 19th-century U.S. senator notoriously put it) "a self-evident lie."[31] How could anyone say that it's obvious that all of us are created equal when the most obvious thing about people is that every one of us is different? Some people are smarter, handsomer, more ethical, of better character. All you have to do is open your eyes. Nor is the Declaration redeemed by arguing that the

---

[31] Sen. John Pettit of Indiana, in the debate over the Kansas and Nebraska Act of 1854.

words are only rhetoric. Empty rhetoric rarely has good results.

Yet perhaps it's even worse. Perhaps the Declaration isn't arguing that all men are equal in any outward manifestations but that we're all equal within — that nobody is any better than anyone else, that we all are deserving of equal respect or love, or whatever the latest chatter of the super-sensitive might be.

But just as we cannot say that everyone is equally handsome or equally smart, on what basis would we say that everyone is equally fine in character or in morals, and therefore that everyone is equally deserving of respect or affection? Why would we want to lump the high with the low or the good in with the bad and cover over serious differences?

Indeed, we should celebrate the fact, conservative Americans especially might say, that we have great men and women — greater than we are — as models: heroic saints to emulate, geniuses to honor, and wise statesmen to respect. To say that children are equal to parents, or Anthony Weiner to George Washington, or any of us to Albert Einstein or Mother Teresa is not only foolish but corrupt. If that's where this idea of "equality" leads us, conservatives have argued, we should repudiate it root and branch.

The principle of equality might have some merit if it spurred us to elevate ourselves, our society, and our entire culture morally and intellectually. But as conservatives have pointed out, equality is always easier to bring about by pushing people and cultures downward: It's easier to make a civilization vulgar than cultured, easier to be ignorant than educated, easier to make the beautiful ugly than the ugly beautiful.

In its most extreme form, this is what Kurt Vonnegut satirized in his story about the government official who made everyone equal by disfiguring the faces of the beautiful and destroying the minds of the more intelligent.[32] This kind of equality of results not only seems unjust, it clearly has terrible social, economic, and cultural consequences as well. It does nothing to promote and reward true merit in anything from sports to culture or art or the life of the mind.

Could it be that this is what Jefferson had in mind when he wrote that "all men are created equal"? It seems impossible.

Finally, conservatives have argued that equality is the very opposite of liberty — that the more equality there is in society, the less freedom. Since most Americans, liberals as well as conservatives, are strong partisans of freedom, perhaps we should simply spurn the idea of equality completely.

* * * * *

So Jefferson gets it from both sides. Liberals point out that what he says about equality is untrue in fact, and some conservatives believe that it might even be untrue in principle!

But Jefferson was hardly a man incapable of seeing the obvious. Of course he and his fellow Founders could see inequalities everywhere around them. Not only inequalities of wealth between the few with great property and the many who were so much poorer, but also inequalities of power, between the colonists and the crown, and — the clearest of inequalities — between freemen and slaves. Still, Jefferson not only could not only pen the words "all men are created equal" but also say that in writing these words he was doing nothing more than echoing the common understanding of the day. All Americans of his generation thought these words were true — even "self-evidently"

---

[32] Kurt Vonnegut, "Harrison Bergeron," 1961.

true. And, I believe, all good Americans should think them true today. *But what on earth is the truth these words are trying to express?*

* * * * *

To figure out what the Declaration means when it says, "all men are created equal," let us begin in a simple and obvious way: For one person to be equal to another means that no one is created subordinate to another. The equality of all men means that no one is my superior by nature. No one — not king, not pope or minister, not nobleman or strongman — is born with any right to make me do his bidding. Even parents, perhaps the closest thing we have to ordinary natural superiors, may not treat their children as their slaves or use them simply for their own purposes.

If all men are created equal, then you may not force me to give up what is rightly mine, or take away from me what I achieve through the use of my talents, or force me to submit to your schemes without my consent. Because "all men are created equal," you may not treat me as if I were your slave; you may not steal from me or kill me or even order me around. I am your equal, not your subordinate.

Despite the fact that Jefferson had slaves, he nonetheless was painfully aware that slavery was unjust. Although we will try to unravel this contradiction later, it must be said up front that if slavery doesn't contradict the core belief of the Declaration then nothing does.

* * * * *

Jefferson's words are, when properly understood, the foundation, the bedrock, of all our rights, of our liberties, and of our American democracy. Because all men are created equal, because there can never be a legitimate claim of "divine right" or any other kind of "right" to rule over us, we are a free nation of free people.

Yes, many people are handsomer or smarter or richer or more moral than you or I might be. In that regard we are clearly and often radically unequal. But because no one is called by God or designed by nature to be my ultimate superior, I am allowed to be myself. I am allowed to choose how I will worship, who my friends are, whether to excel or to slack off, whether to be different or go with the crowd. Above all, I am allowed to choose to live my life by my own lights. And I am so allowed because all men are created equal — no one is my superior by divine decree; no man is my ruler by nature.

Despite the fact that conservatives often say that liberty and equality are "opposite," the truth is that they are, at base and in origin, more like twins, even conjoined twins. The truth of our liberty is self-evident because the truth of our equality is self-evident, no matter how many men may think, or wish, to deny it. We are not "dependent" human beings, as slaves wrongly are, or those who depend for their life and livelihood on the state. We are, as the phrase common in the Founders' time went, "free, equal, and independent."

Reflect on all this for a moment: How are we all equal? Obviously not in wealth or looks or character or intelligence or morals. Some of us are morally better than others, some of us richer, some of us smarter. In those things we are plainly unequal. But we are all equal in regards to the fact that none of us is born either with the right to rule others or with the obligation to bend to others because they say so. We possess "certain unalienable rights" because each of us was "created equal." We have the right to life, to liberty, to property, to protect ourselves, to pursue happiness — to do all that we associate with free men and women. Or, as Jefferson once said so pointedly, "the mass of mankind has not been born with saddles on their backs" nor others "booted and spurred, ready to ride them."[33]

None of this implies that the state should endeavor to *make* persons equal. We have already gotten a glimpse of why that way lies madness and ultimately tyranny. Jefferson wasn't being sloppy in using the word "created." We all are equal from birth and equal in the only way that matters politically: equal in our liberties, equal in our rights not to be lorded over by someone or any group that wishes to command us without our consent.

Yet this does not mean that government has no role to play in our social, moral, or economic lives — that its only job is, as many libertarians might argue, to stay out of the way. At a minimum, government is, as Jefferson immediately points out, actively needed to *secure* our rights. "To secure these rights, Governments are instituted among Men, deriving their just powers from the consent of the governed." This protection of our rights is something every conservative understands: an army and navy to protect our liberties, police and courts to protect our persons and property, and so on.

But the securing of rights hardly means freezing everyone in place. As both liberals and conservatives have long understood, it also means assuring our right to achieve, to increase our property and possessions, and to better our happiness and well being. Government is not established to secure any pretended right

---

[33] With echoes of his Declaration, Jefferson called this idea a "palpable truth." See Jefferson's letter to Roger C. Weightman, June 24, 1826. This was last letter Jefferson wrote.

to the equal possession of the goods of the world. But legitimate government does have a role in helping to secure *equality of opportunity* for all. Or, as Abraham Lincoln, the president who perhaps best understood the full meaning of the Declaration, once said: What Jefferson promised us in 1776 was that "in due time the weights should be lifted from the shoulders of all men, and that *all* should have an equal chance."[34]

Government is also charged with helping protect and promote the conditions under which we can all work to succeed. What American conservatism needs to understand is that, yes, government must be "limited" so not as to *invade* our rights — but it also has an obligation actively to help us *secure* our rights, *protect* our freedoms from both domestic as well as foreign enemies, and *actively support* the increase in the paths of advancement and opportunity so that all men can work out proper avenues of achievement and happiness. It is with this understanding — and not the false view that equality means taking and redistributing, or punishing success and demonizing the successful — that both American conservatives and liberals can, one hopes, find some common ground.

* * * * *

Perhaps it would also be useful to approach the idea of human equality from a different angle — not by looking across and comparing ourselves to our neighbors, but by looking up and down. Most of us agree, for instance, that we can use animals for our purposes: We can use them for companionship, for work, or even for food. We cannot slaughter and harm them needlessly, since that reduces us to their level and degrades our humanity. But we can do what we

---

34 Speech at Independence Hall, February 22, 1861.

reasonably will with them because they are not our equals.

Not many of us would think it dreadful if, coming home from work, our spouse told us he had killed a few chickens and fed them to the kids. Yet every one of us would think it monstrous if he told us that he had slaughtered the children and fed them to the chickens. All humans are equal; but no animal is our equal.

Let's take this a small step further and look up: We are not God's equal. He is superior to us. He can, as believers would attest, bring us into life at His will and call us from it as He determines.

But because all men are created equal, we cannot treat others as if they are animals for our use, nor can we consider ourselves gods, lording over other men. Unless we consent to it for ourselves, both slavery and kingship are illegitimate. As Jefferson said, you and I are not born with saddles on our backs, nor are others born booted and spurred. We cannot treat other people as means to our ends. Nor may others — whether other nations or other individuals – so treat us.

* * * * *

Some commentators (especially those of a more conservative bent) try to reduce the centrality of equality in the Declaration by interpreting equality to mean simply that all men are equal in rights. As they point out, what follows the declaration that "all men are created equal" are the words "that they are endowed by their Creator with certain unalienable rights, that among these are Life, Liberty, and the pursuit of Happiness." So, clearly, there is this intimate connection between our equality and our rights, our individual liberties.

But *we are not equal because we all have rights, we have rights because we are all equal.* We possess "certain unalienable rights" because each of us was "created equal." Because we are all created equal to one another, nothing is more manifest, nothing more palpable, than that you may not kill me for your pleasure, force me to work for your profit, or steal my money or my property for your uses — even if you are wiser, better, handsomer, holier, or stronger.

Even children, because they are equally human, have rights: You, no matter who you are, no matter how rich or powerful or famous, cannot steal even a penny from a schoolchild without doing an injustice. The child may not be your equal in power or age or importance, but he is equal to you in being a human, and so you may not steal from him; you may not treat him, in this way, as your subordinate.

But we also need to recognize that equality is a larger concept than simply the ground of our rights. Some of the most crucial political issues cannot be easily framed in terms of rights and can only be seen through the lens of equality itself. Even the attack on slavery gets muddled if we only see it in terms of "rights" alone. Then we have competing rights — the rights of slaveholders, property rights, states' rights, and so on. Slavery is illegitimate because it's a frontal attack on the notion of human equality — from which the notion of the right to be free inexorably flows — not because one right prevails over another right.

The same is true with abortion. We all know that it can be framed as a conflict of two rights — the right to choose on one side and the right to life on the other. But it makes greater sense to see it in terms of an equality that precedes rights: If human, the child is our equal. We therefore have no arbitrary power over it; we cannot claim any right or desire of ours against it; we cannot use it for our purposes. We cannot willy-nilly kill a child. It is our equal.

Most important, the truth that all men are created equal keeps us from assenting to the greatest heresy of the last two centuries: *that there are gradations of being human.* After Jefferson, we no longer can ever legitimately say that blacks or Jews or those we might consider beneath us are not "fully human." Yes, there are those who would deny the humanity of the unborn child. But if not human, what is it? Half human? On its way to becoming human? We cannot say that the unborn or the young are only in the "process" of becoming real persons. If all men are created equal, then there cannot be any Orwellian step in which some men are more equal, or "more human," than others.

* * * * *

Why make such a big deal out of this notion of equality? Why not talk about other principles first, like liberty or checked and balanced government or federalism? Because for Americans, everything hinges on this one idea. This is why Jefferson put it first, why Lincoln always spoke about it. And why all Americans on all parts of the political spectrum have to respect it and appreciate it: In political life, it is the ground of our liberties and the impetus behind our democracy; in our social and family life, it shapes our understanding and colors our conduct. And in our moral life, it defines the very contours of what is just and what is not.

Yet the most dangerous threat to our liberties as Americans today stems from a flawed and erroneous understanding of equality. Some, as we have seen, think it means leveling — taking from those who have "too much" and redistributing it to others. Some think of equality not as equal rights and equality before the law, but as equality of possessions, equality of "results," and various kinds of preferential treatment. Some would have government rewarding individuals simply on the basis of their race or gender while denying the same benefit or opportunity to others of the "wrong" race or sex. Some would sooner see equality at the expense of freedom than a society where some rise and others fall and where some have more or less than others. These are the people who have truly made liberty and equality opposites.

Equality and the Totalitarian Impulse

We need always to remind ourselves that the Founders knew that people were not equal in outward manifestations or achievements or possessions. More particularly, they knew that we could not be made equal in such things without tyrannical force. How ferocious, how terrifying, has been the history of the last century, which saw some of the worst crimes against humanity stemming from the desire to enforce the idea that all should be "made" equal. Though we will never have an exact count, in China, the Soviet Union, Cambodia, and North Korea, perhaps upwards of 100 million people perished in crusades to "make" people equal.

It may seem paradoxical, but it is true nonetheless: *equality leads to freedom, and this freedom leads inexorably to differences of wealth, accomplishments, and honor.* A society that understands the equality of all people and respects the equal right of everyone to follow his own lights and exercise her own talents *will always be a society that has an inequality of results*, where men and women rise to different social, economic, and educational levels. And the attempt to force an equality of results is the mark of an unjust and tyrannical society.[35]

We can be a society that ensures equality of opportunity and equality of rights — with all the diversity and differences that flow from such equality — or we can be a nation that tries to impose equality of result. We cannot be both.

Although the idea of equality should chasten liberals and progressives rather than embolden them, this shouldn't give conservatives encouragement to be on the side of the rich or powerful or privileged. Real conservatism is not a front for aristocracy; it doesn't shill for the powerful. Real conservatism does everything it can to keep the avenues of economic and social achievement open. It especially rejects the notion of government collusion with the already well off to retard the rise of new entrepreneurs, new businesses, new inventors. Real conservatism does all it can to open up avenues of opportunity to rise, prosper, and be our unique selves. Real conservatism understands that because all men are created equal, neither a socialism that looks to equalize the fruits of our labors and talents, nor an aristocracy that pretends it can take whatever it wishes, are ever just.

* * * * *

The self-evident truth proclaimed in our Declaration of Independence — that all men are created equal — not only leads us better to understand the meaning of rights, it also helps us understand the basis of all

---

[35] Consider, again, Prof. Rawls: Our modern and egalitarian conception of social justice will "put limits on which satisfactions have value; they impose restrictions on what are reasonable conceptions of one's good," *A Theory of Justice*, p.31, sec. 6. "A just social system defines the scope within which individuals must develop their aims, and it provides a framework of rights and opportunities and the means of satisfaction within and by the use of which these ends may be equitably pursued," Ibid. A clearer description of the connection between modern egalitarian "justice" and the totalitarian impulse would be hard to imagine.

just government. Because of our natural equality one with another, all legitimate government derives its just powers "from the consent of the governed."

Although this principle of the Declaration might seem obvious to Americans today — that the people always have the last word in who should be governing them — it surely hasn't been obvious throughout history or even to much of the world today. For most of the world's history there have been raging fights over who should have the last word, and "the people" was rarely the answer. Perhaps, some have said, the wise should rule — perhaps "philosopher kings." Or perhaps the good should rule. How better to have a decent and just country? Or perhaps, above all, God should rule — and if He is otherwise occupied, no doubt his representatives on earth should tell us how to live.

All of these have had a claim to being the best rule. Some men have always and everywhere treated other men as subordinates or animals, as if the mass of people were merely the means for fulfilling the wishes of the few. But history does not dictate morality to nature. The Declaration of Independence doesn't say that subordination isn't a fact of political life. It merely states the *moral* claim that such a history doesn't make the claim just.

The Declaration says that it is *only through popular consent* that anyone who possesses any of these attributes — intelligence, goodness, respect for God's will — is justified in ruling. If the people want to have the best person in the country as their president — perhaps George Washington — they can. But not even George Washington can claim to be president *by right*.

Washington understood this. In declining to even consider being king, he knew not only how central to our rights but also how necessary for the future of popular government everywhere was this formative idea of the equality of all men.

- II -

Economics and Justice

ADAM SMITH PUBLISHED *The Wealth of Nations* in 1776, the same year as our own Declaration of Independence. This was a coincidence — but not completely. Political liberty and economic liberty go hand in hand, and America was born at a time when the ties between political and economic principles were becoming clearer. Indeed, the rise of modern economics actually made modern liberal democracy possible.

* * * * *

We say these days, far too cavalierly, that economics is a central and even deciding factor in life. "It's the economy, stupid." Your outlook, how you will vote, your behavior will all reflect either your current economic status or your desire to get ahead financially. Thus, we are told, rich people will vote Republican, and poor people Democratic.

Now, we know this isn't true. The rich in America are often the most liberal, and the poor and middle classes often highly conservative. Connecticut votes for Democrats and Mississippi for Republicans. There's so much more in our lives than just our wallets and our bank accounts that shape our outlook: our religious beliefs and values, our education and experience.

But there is a serious way in which, when it comes to politics, it *is* the economy. Whether the people are ferociously poor and without hope of advancement, or are rising in prosperity and in their ability to satisfy the needs of their families, makes all the difference for the success of democratic government.

Before the coming of the modern era, the vast majority of people were poor. Not poor by the standards of modern affluence but truly, desperately, poor — at best, just a few steps from squalor and starvation. Nor were there many ways out. Kings and clergy had control of what little wealth there was, and the poor and their children had little hope for any kind of real material advancement.

"The poor" and "the vast majority" were, in times past, virtually synonymous. Aristotle, that great philosopher of ancient Greece, fluctuates between calling democracy the rule of the majority and the rule of the poor. No one back then would have thought this odd.

But this poverty causes a serious problem for democratic government. If the poor rule, then no one's property or possessions are secure. It's not that the poor are necessarily bad — it's that they're needy. This combination of need and political power means that anyone who has possessions holds them very insecurely when the government is a democracy.

Before the 17th century, there were a few attempts to forge democratic or more specifically "republican" governments, and some of these (Athens and especially Rome come to mind) were successful and occasionally long lasting. But in these and other successful attempts we most often see democracy as only a part of the government. The Roman Republic lasted for centuries by "balancing" — playing off, in a sense — the poor against the upper classes, forcing both to agree before legislation could be passed. But while these "mixed" governments often worked — think also of the mix of king, lords, and commons in England — purely popular or democratic nations rarely succeeded.[36]

---

[36] See Hamilton in *Federalist*, No. 9: "It is impossible to read the history of the petty republics of Greece and Italy without feeling sensations of horror and dis-

So the first problem that poverty poses to any kind of potential democracy is that poverty leads to a whole raft of unpleasant consequences. The rich, in order to retain their status, have to keep the poor down; the poor, often in order simply to survive, have to take what they can. Rights are violated on all sides; laws are severe and punishments often capital; and revolutions are frequent and bloody.

But today — *at least where modern commerce has taken hold* — when we hear the word "minority" we no longer think of the few rich but, rather, the few poor! Unlike in Aristotle's time, in today's developed countries the words "poor" and "minority" have become virtually synonymous. This means that the very character of democracy has changed. Without the desperately poor and revolutionary in the majority, perhaps for the first time we can hope for stability in democratic government.

There's more. Once we have found a way through the encouragement and protection of free markets of *increasing* wealth in society and not just *redistributing* it, once we have found a way to make the majority of people middle class rather than poor, we will have both increased comfort and general well-being and also made domestic politics far more peaceful, far less turbulent. *A society where people can earn more by working than by taking is a happier, more placid, less rapacious, more secure, and by any measure more just society than was ever in centuries past thought possible.*

Finally, if a way can be found to increase this societal prosperity by freeing men rather than by directing or controlling them, then a true, happy, and almost

---

gust at the distractions with which they were continually agitated, and at the rapid succession of revolutions by which they were kept in a state of perpetual vibration between the extremes of tyranny and anarchy."

miraculous advance in political and social life has oc-
curred. Explaining this miracle is where John Locke —
Adam Smith's philosophical English forebear —
comes in.

The American Revolution has any number of important political philosophers behind it, but none was
more important than Locke. Locke was an English
physician, a philosopher and psychologist, and an
economic and political theorist of the first rank. So
alive were the ideas in his books to our Founders that
Jefferson took parts of Locke's *Second Treatise of
Government* and put them verbatim into the Declaration of Independence. My guess is that he didn't go
back to see what he had underlined in his copy of the
Treatise — no doubt Jefferson had Locke's words,
phrases, and ideas known (as we used to say) "by
heart."

How is it, Locke has us ask, that we all have things
we call our own? Where, that is, do we get the right to
property? We might respond, "It's a God-given right,"
but that's a hard thing to prove, especially to those
who have no belief in God. And even those who believe in God sometimes like to think that the goods of
this world were given to everybody, that we all have a
right to everything, that socialism or communism is
the "more Christian" way, and that (as one philosopher famously said) private property is theft.

Still, everyone knows or at least should be able to
sense that, if we "own" little else, we at least own ourselves. But if we own ourselves, we own what we do
with ourselves; we own our labor. My exertion, the
work of my hands, is no one's but mine. If I find a
pretty stone in the forest or I collect nuts off the
ground or I pick an apple from a tree in the wilderness
that no one else has any claim to, these objects are
mine. They can't be anyone else's.

Now it could surely be argued that if you picked all the apples in the wilderness so that no one else could ever have any, they are not all yours. You cannot take everything so that all others starve. They, too, have an equal right to life and to the fruits of their labor, and you have no warrant to take those rights away. But suppose I picked a number of apples, even more than I could use, and traded a few of them for nuts that someone else picked? Now we have both benefited, and we both are eating better than if we had to subsist on nuts or apples alone. I did have to work harder to get a few extra bushels of apples for trade, but my labor is paying off for both me and my neighbors. My picking more apples than I could eat not only didn't hurt my neighbors, we all benefitted from my extra exertions.

Now, suppose, rather than waiting till autumn comes and scurrying around madly to pick as many apples as I can to trade for less perishable goods to keep me alive for another year, I decide to enclose some bare and uncultivated ground and plant apple trees? Yes, this is extra work for me, but in time the result — thanks to my digging and planting and pruning and fertilizing — is more apples, and probably better quality apples. My apples, now traded for nuts and milk and grain and eggs, are helping to feed many more. I have, through my exertions, benefited me and greatly benefitted my neighbors as well. Indeed, what was fallow land before, with a few scraggly and fairly unproductive trees, is now an expansive and productive orchard. And the land that once gave, say, 10 bushels of apples now produces a hundred, or a thousand times more.

So, what have my labors accomplished? Certainly something for me — I can now trade the apples that I now have in abundance for a cornucopia of good things for me and my family. But even more: *By the use of my private property, I have created an increase in goods more generally.* Rather than "theft," my enclosing and subsequent farming of my own orchard has benefitted the whole society. My private property increased the well being of everyone. Yes, I am now rich. I even trade some of my superabundance of apples for that pretty metal I saw, and I save it since it never rots or gets wormy. And I use this gold or silver to buy whatever I want from others who also fancy the shiny stuff. But my wealth, all gotten by free exchange, has harmed no one and truly benefitted many.

Now, all this may seem like a silly story, a fable or a myth, but Locke offers it to us so that we can understand that something like this happens all the time when we free ourselves from the notion that everybody has a right to everything, or that social ownership is better than private ownership, or that somehow private property is low or un-Christian or destructive of our better natures. In fact, Locke wants us to understand that *a respect for the right of private property is the beginning of social — not simply individual — prosperity.*

Yes, wanting to get ahead materially in this world may not look like the most high-minded thing. It may not seem noble or spiritual. But while railing against "materialism" or "consumerism" may make the speaker feel virtuous, his view is not only not charitable but also downright nasty. There is no doubt that the A&P has fed more poor souls than all the sanctimonious sentiments of the communal and self-righteous throughout all history. It wasn't politics that contributed to the general wellbeing of all, nor was it preaching about "sharing" or a central-command economy, nor was it even pious sermons about charity or living like field lilies. What brought about the abundance (yes, *abundance*) we see all around us, and what ultimately helped make modern democracy possible, was the development of an economic system that freed people to make, cultivate, build, and invent — in brief, to pursue freely their own material interests as they themselves thought best.[37]

Equality has led us to freedom, and freedom has led us to prosperity. And these allowed the Founders to construct a democratic government that has lasted for over two centuries.

Free people to be themselves, free them to follow their desires to advance and get ahead in this world, and good things ensue for all.

This is why *making and increasing* the wealth and goods of this world is more important than redistribution. So long as avenues of opportunity are open to all and there is no collusion between those in power to undercut the equal opportunity of all to rise and to fall, then not only does the existence of wealth in others' hands not hurt me, it often benefits me. That this singer or that sports figure or this inventor or that entrepreneur has millions does me little harm — except maybe to my pride — and will actually provide me with far greater enjoyment, more comfort, and heightened material productivity than if everyone were equally poor.

---

[37] This is also why such statements as "you didn't build it" seem both factually false as well as theoretically so misguided. Indeed, it is pretty much *only* the independent exertions of free people who build *anything*. Even the roads over which goods are brought to market (to use one of the examples of how "government" helped build your business) were paved with asphalt mixes developed by individual enterprise, delivered by trucks and front-end loaders built by private companies, and finished by workmen recruited and paid by private firms. Unless we're talking about Cuba or North Korea, when it comes to getting a job done, governments need private enterprise and open markets far more than the other way around.

* * * * *

We humans "thirst for justice," as the Bible says. But we rarely seem to agree on what justice *is*. Is executing a criminal justice or vengeance? Is "an eye for an eye" just, or are we called to "rehabilitate" malefactors? Many people think enforced "equality" or sharing everything "equally" is more just than letting people keep and enjoy the fruits of their own labor. On the other side, some on the libertarian right believe that all taxation is a form of unjust taking and that individual liberty allows little room for civic obligations or economic regulation. So, between the egalitarians and redistributionists on one side and radical individualists on the other (not to mention all the rest of us in between!), everything seems to be up for grabs when it comes to notions of justice.

To put it differently, while it might be said that justice means giving people what they deserve, what exactly people "deserve" is always disputed. Still, most people seem not to have a problem in arguing that workers must get paid for their labor, that wounded soldiers should get excellent medical care, and that parents must feed and clothe their children. Parents who do not feed their children commit, in our minds, a monstrous injustice.

So, it's not that we, as humans, lack a general notion or core conception of justice. For an employer to break his word or his contract with his employees is generally an injustice and everybody knows it. No one disagrees that stealing from the poor or taking advantage of the most vulnerable is unjust. But when it comes to taking from the not-so-poor, or placing special penalties on those some think of as "privileged," well, then, we do begin to have some rather serious disagreements.

But let's look at the problem of what's "deserved" from a slightly different angle. There is still another kind of justice that requires that we do what we can to repay those who have done great things for us. Who doesn't sense that it is altogether right and just that national heroes be honored with celebrations, great saints with feast days, soldiers with parades and medals, and great scholars with academic acclaim? But liberal capitalism, the free market, has found a pretty good way of honoring not saints and scholars but those who make, produce, invent, and deliver. It gives them money. Sometimes lots and lots of money. With which they can buy fine houses, gold watches, the richest foods, hire servants, secure the finest medical care ... whatever they fancy. They can even take their money and make more money, if that makes them happy.

This particular way of allocating money and goods bothers more than a few people in our world (especially those who see themselves as more saintly and more scholarly!). Yes, some people have more than others. But so long as we have an economic system that rewards rather than penalizes those who labor, who produce, and who add to the store of our goods and enjoyment, then we have a system that is as close to justice as most of us understand it as we might get. Under the form of liberal capitalism we have today, goods and services are produced beyond the wildest dreams of antiquity, so that the poor, through their efforts, can become far less poor and the lowly became far less low. We in the developed world have an abundance of goods, entertainments, medicines; we have the ability to travel, advance, and educate ourselves and our children; we have the satisfaction of needs and the enjoyment of luxuries unknown and unimaginable to previous ages.

Of course, if the rich are rewarded for doing evil — theft, Ponzi schemes, monopolistic practices, gouging — then society has every right to correct the problem and repair the system again. Economics may have come to the aid of politics in helping to solve the problem of justice and material production, but it didn't eliminate the need for politics, statesmanship, and an intelligent and rational public. Believing that modern free enterprise has given amazing blessings to the world is not the same as believing that free enterprise should never be regulated or that it should be "unfettered."

At the same time, to believe that "unfettered capitalism" is at the root of the ills of the world — grinding poverty, disease, wars, terrorism, torture, you name it — is to believe in an evil that *nowhere exists* while overlooking the true evils in the world: fanaticism, religious zealotry, greed un-channeled into enterprise, envy, resentment, racial and tribal or ethnic hatred, and so on. In fact, a healthy dose of capitalism might just help mitigate many of these real causes of human misery!

In former times, such people who yearned for distinction or power — firebrands, demagogues, would-be tyrants — posed a constant danger to democracies. Modern economics hasn't eliminated or overcome the natural ambitions of men any more than moral preaching or fine sermons ever did. But modern economics has certainly helped turn the attention of ambitious men to more positive and productive activities. As so many of the zealots of the 1960's learned, there's a lot more to be gained in business than in occupying the library. Or, as Samuel Johnson long ago observed, a man rarely acts more innocently than when he's engaged in making money.

So it seems that our free-market system has done an amazing thing: It has raised the general well being of all society so that the poor are no longer many but few. In doing this, it eased the problem faced by all previous democracies — the impossibility of establishing a stable and just polity through the empowering of the rapacious and revolutionary poor. Now, all have property to defend, all have "a stake" in the stability and protection of society. It is now possible to understand that gain through productive labor is better than gain through taking. Moreover, it helps satisfy our sense of justice — both justice to the poor and justice to the hard working and productive. And, finally, it helps turn those who might wish to rule in order to satisfy their lust for gain, for conquest, or for power into more socially useful and productive channels.

* * * * *

This is all well and good, you might say, but it hardly helps with this or that policy decision. How does recognizing the validity of what John Locke and Adam Smith said help us decide whether or not to raise the debt ceiling or expand or constrict Social Security or empower the Food and Drug Administration or increase the FDIC's role in guaranteeing our savings? And, to an extent, this criticism is reasonable. As we noted in the introduction, the Founders' understanding is often less a set of commandments than a way of thinking, a mindset for approaching problems.

Nonetheless, let's not give away too much. General rules are indispensable for both figuring out the right policy path to take and which paths to avoid. A person who understands the aims and the virtues of a free-market economy will always look askance at any scheme to redistribute wealth from the more productive to the more envious, sometimes even to the more needy. Yes, there are times when society demands that those unable to be productive — orphans, the sick, the mentally ill — need societal support. But he will not be beguiled by sentimental phrases that try to embarrass him into undermining an economic system that has produced more goods and services, raised more people from abject poverty, fought disease and warded off premature death more than any other economic system, no matter how "fair" the other side may try to portray itself.

"Social justice" and "fairness" are indeed a kind of "justice." But it's not an American form of justice. And it has precious little to do with justice as the Founders understood it.

On this point, let's be as clear as we can: To our Founders, justice and "fairness" lay not in distributing the goods and benefits of society to all people equally. The Founders' justice does not envision a "more equal" redistribution of wealth simply because we are all born equally human. Rather, true social justice demands that people be allowed to possess what they earn, and enjoy the fruits of their own individual exertions. To take from the inventive, the hard working, the productive, and even the lucky what they have is unjust to the worker and maker. It is, moreover, unjust to society since anything that depresses the incentive to produce reduces the wealth, health, and prosperity of the nation as a whole.

"The first object of government," Madison tells us in *The Federalist Papers*, is "the protection of different and unequal faculties of acquiring property."[38] Madison understood that this would result in "the possession of different degrees and kinds of property." In a free country where all men are equal and where

---

[38] *Federalist*, No. 10.

rights are protected by government, some will wind up richer and others poorer. But it is *the first object* of just government to protect those rights and unequal outcomes, not to erase the different abilities of people or to undo the result of our different abilities, imaginations, or efforts.

* * * * *

Before we end this chapter, let's make one final observation on capitalism and democracy. Perhaps the most interesting thing about the free market is that it creates all that it does from very ordinary materials. It's "democratic" to its core. We've all heard it said, "Students who earn A's go to law school so that they can work for students who made C's." And, in some real measure, it's true. The success of the free market is not the success of geniuses or the supremely capable, but the success of ordinary people doing ordinary tasks well. The free market, liberal capitalism, takes ordinary people with ordinary ambitions — to make some money, to feed and house one's family, to be honored in the community — and turns these ordinary desires into widespread productive good.

As Adam Smith made perfectly clear, society advances in wealth and comfort not because of the benevolence of the butcher, the brewer, or the baker but because each person is more or less following his own interests. This is, in a sense, the "miracle" of the market brought about by modern liberty: Even those who are doing nothing more than seeking their own gain can contribute to the general welfare, the common good. It wasn't to give apples to schoolchildren that Locke's farmer planted his orchard — it was to better the condition of himself and his family.

Even our vices — our self-regard, our hopes for advancement, our desire for comfort and shelter, yes, even our greed — can redound to the public good. The miracle of America is that ordinary people, with ordinary desires and hopes, can both advance themselves and benefit their neighbors at the same time.

This "democratic" miracle gives an open field to everyone, not just to the super-smart, or to the rich, or to those born to the "right" families. It allows all men the ability to better themselves by their own efforts and not be beholden to the state or the collective for their wellbeing. In the many years I spent in the Middle East, it was most depressing to see good people with good minds and hearts hope for "a government job" where the rewards were minimal but the risks non-existent. Even worse, they all expected government handouts for all the everyday things in life. They wanted little more than a higher power to feed them, give them housing, free education, and medical care. They worked for little but felt entitled to everything. This soft bondage to government is hardly productive of democratic, self-governing, free citizens. In fact, the people I met in Iraq who had not spent time in the West seemed, too often, not to have the souls of free people at all. What a tragic thing to say.

Modernity's ability to draw good out of our ordinary human desires is a construct that our Founding Fathers applied to politics and government at a number of different levels, not simply to economics. It is the essence of freedom and the greatness of freedom: to give ordinary human passions and desires more or less free rein, then have them work not only for the benefit of the individual but also for all society.

* * * * *

My analysis of economics and politics in this chapter can fairly be labeled "conservative," but it is hardly "libertarian." Though faithful to Locke, to Smith, and to the Founders, my argument is not simply that "private property is your God-given right," and that "any regulation of your right to private property is unjust." I have *not* made the silly argument that "all taxation is stealing." I have *not* tried to take a philosophy of living and of governing and turned it into an ideology, where all answers are easily given in sound-bite phrases. All Americans — conservatives and liberals — are called to be thoughtful, not to have a set of pre-cut phrases or slogans that we think will answer every serious political question. Nothing could be further from the spirit of the Founders, who deliberated for four months in Philadelphia in 1787, than thinking that pat answers cover all questions. Our American principles are rich and deep, not simple or shallow. The Constitution is not a list of slogans.

Our Founding Fathers were not "libertarians." Yes, they were fully and wholeheartedly on the side of human liberty; securing the "Blessings of Liberty" was central to their idea of constitutional government. But they never argued that liberty and rights were all there were to just government. Nor did they believe that our rights — including the pivotal right to property — were in any way "absolute."

Both Locke's and Smith's highest defense of private property hinges on the truth that it is a grand and magnificent *social* good. Free markets lead to prosperity for many, abundance more widely spread around. If private property has the exact opposite effect — if a few landowners control all the land, or if the means of production are not simply in private hands but in only a few private hands, with all others excluded — then the justification for private property ceases. We cannot dam up the river and call all water ours. Private property is right not only because it rewards your labors and satisfies your personal needs, but because it leads to public, widespread, increase and abundance. If it doesn't, then the people have a right to look for other arrangements. This is why Adam Smith can say that it is the obligation of government to break up monopolies, even though monopolies are, to be sure, the private property of a few. Or, as Locke would observe, because we are all created equal and, therefore, all with an equal right to life and security, we have to understand that our ownership cannot lead to the denial of life or safety for the rest.

This is one place where today's liberals and today's conservatives should be able to agree — the comfort and goods of this world should be more widely enjoyed; the poor and the middle classes should be aided, not hindered, in their quest to be economically more secure; opportunities to become richer and more productive should be constantly advanced; ownership and property increased; and, if there is any "leveling" to be done, the nation should look for every opportunity to help the poor raise themselves up and not simply spend every effort to tear down those who have.

There are still those who see poverty as some kind of virtue and the possession of money as akin to wickedness. There are those who would be happy if all the rich were laid low and the poor admired for their blessedness. But these outlooks are almost certainly counterproductive to both the future of democratic government or the progress of human happiness. Or, to summarize the main points of this chapter: The new science of free enterprise economics has helped bring about not only individual gratification and helped increase the wealth of all nations, it has also gone far to make democracy for the first time a possibility not only in America but elsewhere in the modern world.

- III -

Democracy

EVER NOTICE HOW some of the worst countries in the world proudly call themselves "republics" or "democracies"? Pakistan, Zimbabwe, Venezuela, Sudan and South Sudan, China, Cuba, Iran, Ethiopia, Russia. ... The list of corrupt and oppressive "democracies" is sometimes simply astonishing.

There was a time, not all that long ago, when every schoolchild learned that not every country calling itself a "democracy" or a "republic" was worthy of the name. Every schoolchild once knew that our democratic revolution, which culminated in national independence and a democratic Constitution, was good — but that the highly democratic French Revolution, for example, which culminated in the Terror and the guillotine, was bad. We knew that Red China called itself a democracy, and that the Soviet Union was a union of so-called republics. We also knew that the worst even went so far as to call themselves "peoples' democracies," as if a tautology would somehow excuse their crimes. (For some reason, North Korea thinks that combining everything into one grand trifecta — "The Democratic People's Republic of Korea" — makes it the most special. Perhaps, in a sad way, it does.)

Strangely enough, some of the people least smitten with the superiority of democracy were the Founders themselves. To be sure, they agreed with Jefferson that (since all men were created equal) all legitimate government has to rest on "the consent of the governed," that people could not be ruled without their agreement. And, yes, the Founders did surely give us a fundamentally democratic constitution — a government "of the people, by the people, and for the people," as Lincoln would later characterize it.

Yet neither the Declaration of Independence nor the Constitution ever calls this new nation a "democracy." And while I think we can say that, in the end, the Founders were pleased with the kind of restrained democracy they created — let's characterize it as a "representative" or, better, constitutional democracy — the fact is they were not friends of democracy in general. Today we Americans would do well to look twice at what the Founders saw and be careful about our regard for democracy. We should be especially careful of any and all attempts to spread "democracy" around the world.

Why isn't democratic government simply the best or always desirable? The Founders were careful students of history. And they thought that virtually every example of more or less democratic states throughout history was defective. Alexander Hamilton, in one of *The Federalist Papers*, noted that the republics of antiquity were nations whose histories could only be read with "horror and disgust."[39] James Madison was a bit less vociferous about it, yet even he was compelled to remind us that the evils of "instability, injustice, and confusion" have been "the mortal diseases under which popular governments have everywhere perished."[40]

Of course, all forms of government are problematic. Those who live in monarchies have to worry about the

---

[39] *Federalist,* No. 9. In full, Hamilton notes, "It is impossible to read the history of the petty republics of Greece and Italy without feeling sensations of horror and disgust at the distractions with which they were continually agitated, and at the rapid succession of revolutions by which they were kept in a state of perpetual vibration between the extremes of tyranny and anarchy." Even the small republics recommended by the renowned Montesquieu prompted Hamilton to label them "the wretched nurseries of unceasing discord and the miserable objects of universal pity or contempt."

[40] *Federalist,* No. 10.

king becoming a tyrant; those who live under aristocratic rule have to fear the exploitation of the common people by the ruling classes. In theocracies, one has to worry about fire and the stake. But in democracies, the problem is chaos, ignorance, and injustice. Even if every Athenian were a Socrates, Madison goes so far as to say, every Athenian assembly would still be a mob![41]

The Founders had dozens of historical examples of democratic or popular governments devolving into chaos, then being conquered by foreign enemies or taken over by a powerful faction or a demagogue.[42] They had dozens of examples of "the people" being swayed by their emotions, or their ignorance, or by the encouragement of sweet-tongued rabble-rousers.[43] Think, for a moment, of the most awful scene of democracy run wild, a scene pointedly familiar to every American during the Founders' time. Think about the trial and death not of Socrates but of Christ.

Who demanded that Jesus be killed? The people. All the people? No, but definitely a great mob of them. Who egged them on? Well, those highly placed people who had an interest in seeing Jesus dead — the chief priests, the religious leaders of the day. They riled up the crowd and the crowd demanded his death. What was this same crowd doing earlier that week when Jesus first came to town? They sang to him, and put their coats on the ground where he was traveling; they treated him like the greatest hero ever. And within five days they were yelling their heads off that he

---

[41] *Federalist*, No. 55.

[42] The "turbulent democracies of ancient Greece and modern Italy," as Madison referred to them. *Federalist*, No. 14.

[43] "What bitter anguish," Madison writes, "would not the people of Athens have often escaped if their government had contained so provident a safeguard against the tyranny of their own passions." *Federalist*, No. 63.

should die a horrible, inhuman death. They even said they wanted a thief freed and Jesus killed, even though Jesus was until recently their favorite person and best friend. That was the image of democratic rule that many Americans had in the back of their minds.

Still, it wasn't simply the insanity or volatility that came with democratic rule that bothered the Founders, bad as they might be. What bothered them most was *the tendency of democracies to proclaim liberty on the one hand and to undermine it on the other*. After the Revolution the colonies, upon becoming states, took on all the attributes — and all the weaknesses — of democracies in general. And it was the active violations of liberty and individual rights taking place in the newly freed states that, as much as anything, propelled us to discard our first quasi-constitution, the Articles of Confederation, and write the Constitution itself.

The most glaring problems of the Articles of Confederation included a lack of sufficient defense against foreign dangers, the inadequate regulation of commerce, and the inability to raise regular revenue. But even more important was "the necessity of providing for the security of private rights and the steady dispensation of Justice." "Interferences with these," Madison noted, "were evils which perhaps more than anything else, produced this [Federal] convention. Was it to be supposed that republican liberty could long exist under the abuses of it practiced in some of the States."[44]

---

[44] Madison's speech in the Federal Convention on June 6, 1787, in Max Farrand, ed., *The Records of the Federal Convention of 1787*, four volumes, Volume I, p. 134 (New Haven: Yale University Press 1937, 1966). As should become clearer as we go on, hard-line conservatives should remind themselves of these and similar comments by the Founders before they give any full-bore defense of "states' rights."

We should remind ourselves that the Founders, un-like so many of us today, never saw democracy as an end in itself. Rather, the real ends of political life are justice, peace, security, prosperity, and freedom. And it was exactly because these are the goals of political life that the Founders were so careful with democracy. And even though people often lump "democracy" and "liberty" together, there was not then nor had there ever been before anything to connect simple democ-ratic rule, rule "by the people," with justice or peace or, above all, freedom.[45]

So what the Founding Fathers had to do was set up a democracy that wasn't like any of the other democ-racies. It had to be "of the people, by the people, and for the people" — but it had to be sensible. It couldn't be mob rule or the kind of government where a rab-ble-rouser or smooth talker could whip up the country to follow him or give him extraordinary powers. Above all, it had to be a democracy that actually did protect our rights and not violate them.

Of course, "We, the people" could have consented to any form of governing we thought suited us best. But we could not and would not re-establish a king to rule us as in Britain and most other Western coun-tries. After all, we had only recently fought a war to throw off George III. Nor would America ever consent to be ruled by this or that social or economic class. Even though all of classical political science held that aristocracies were more stable, more intelligent, and better governed than democracies, we would never

---

[45] To preview a bit of what will be argued later, so fundamentally successful were the Founders in changing and moderating our brand of democracy that, in the past 50 years, there was hardly an American anywhere who didn't think that "democracy" and "freedom" were simply the same thing — that democracy *meant* freedom. How disabused we were of this error when, in trying mightily to estab-lish democracies abroad, we often found that the more democratic nations be-came, the less free, less liberal, and less just they also became. But more on this anon.

trust any class of people to rule over us. Nor, to be sure, would we ever consent to theocratic rule — to be governed by bishops, or elders, or anything like a pope.

By 1787, when the Founders wrote our Constitution, we probably could not be anything other than a democratic republic. Over the years we had already developed democratic habits, we had our own colonial legislatures, and, above all, we knew that the people were the true basis of government, not a king or any faction or part of the people — that all legitimate political power comes from "the consent of the governed." So the task before the Founders was not to invent democracy but to find ways of making this historically challenging form of government — "democracy" — work here in America.

Americans today have become quite blasé about democracy. Actively or passively, we try to plant democracy everywhere in the world, even in the most backward, intolerant, and fanatical places. We began the 20th century with the hope that our actions — joining a world war — would "make the world safe for democracy." And we began the 21st century with another war waged in the name of democracy. What we didn't understand then or now was that the Founders had no interest in making the world safe for democracy. If anything, their goal was almost opposite — to make democracy safe for the world. That would hardly be a small task, and they knew it.

The next three chapters — on liberty, on the structure of constitutional government, and on the character of Americans — are crucial for understanding what the Founders wanted to achieve and how they went about doing it. But let's take a moment here to understand what the Founders did not do.

First, in setting up a fundamentally democratic government, as they did, they did not rely on the "goodness of the people" or any such romantic notions of human nature to support it. Not one of the Founders would have agreed with Rousseau that men were fundamentally good and only society or the love of possessions corrupted them. But I do not believe the Founders had any different a view of humanity than most of us do. People are a mix of good and bad, altruism and selfishness, neighborliness and nastiness. This is true of both society as a whole and each of us individually — we are all a mix of good and bad, virtue and vice, with some of us better and surely some worse.

Now there were some believers in democratic government — Thomas Paine came close —who thought that a simple reliance on "the people" was enough. But the Founders knew almost instinctively that the part of us that was selfish and self-interested could easily win out over our better selves. Indeed, in some of the newly independent American states, which were each little democracies in their own way, "debtors have defrauded their creditors. The landed interest has borne hard on the mercantile interest. The Holders of one species of property have thrown a disproportion of taxes on the holders of another species."[46] In other words, self-interest had allowed the majority in a democracy to take full advantage of the minority. Or, as Madison put it, "The lesson we are to draw from the whole is that where a majority are united by a common sentiment, and have an opportunity, the rights of

---

[46] *Records*, op. cit. Volume 1, pp. 135-36.

the minor party become insecure."[47] So, simple democracy was out of the question.

Nor did the Founders give in to the idea that if we only pushed the idea of equality to its limit — redistributing wealth and making people more or less equal in their possessions, for instance — that we could then get rid of envy and those desires that led to societal strife. Such equality was not only impossible to achieve in practice, it was undesirable at every level. It would require the suppression of all individual ambition, it would run against that proper individualism that was part of our human natures, and it would mean the destruction of the very liberty that government was meant to protect.

No, if democracy were to succeed, it would have to take our nature, with all its good and bad aspects, into account. The true friends of democracy would need to learn to work with people as they are in fact and not as we might wish them to be.

Romantic democrats might object that this only meant that we need to try harder — to find ways to raise people up, appeal to their consciences, or tap into their innate honesty. Perhaps we could trust people, rather than always assume the worst, and educate them. ("Education" is often the hope of people who have never been educators and never seen first hand its serious limitations.)

Or perhaps we could simply strengthen the role of religion and have a decent society that would be good and just. Reinforce morality, preach the golden rule, and exhort people to remember what God expects of them.

---

[47] Ibid., p. 136. This speech of Madison's at the Federal Convention on June 6 was perhaps the best summary given by any of the Founders of the problems America faced in establishing the new Constitution.

To all of these — education, exhortation, religion — the ever-realistic Founders basically said, don't be silly. Even religion, the binding force of so many previous republics, was itself problematic in this type of new democracy. As Madison publicly noted, "Religion itself may become a motive to persecution and oppression."[48]

So the Founders had to do the most difficult thing: They had to fashion a just and free democracy, where, as Madison says, "neither moral nor religious motives can be relied on."[49] They had to take ordinary fallen and self-interested people and let us rule a great nation, and yet make sure that our rule is decent and fair. In other words, they did what, in the history of politics is the most difficult thing — to combine democratic rule with moderation, good sense, and a respect for freedom.

It had never before been done.

---

[48] Ibid., p. 135.

[49] *Federalist*, No. 10.

- IV -

Liberty

IF WE ASKED a sample of politically aware Americans, "Where do we get our rights?" most would probably say, "from the Bill of Rights." Further, if you asked them "What protects or guarantees our rights?" an equal number would probably say, "the Supreme Court."

Not only are both answers wrong, they are seriously wrong. The Bill of Rights was put together by James Madison, the Father of our Constitution, and became part of the Constitution very soon after we ratified it. But as wonderful as it is, Americans do not get their basic rights from the Constitution, nor from any part of it. As every Founder knew without hesitation, we possess our most basic rights before any government is created or before any political document is ever written. As Jefferson tells us in the Declaration, it is to "secure" our rights that "governments are instituted among men." Rights come first. And not only do governments come second, they exist, in great part, to help us live in the security and possession of these pre-existing rights.

Living before government in what John Locke called "the state of nature" might sound quite carefree and happy — picking acorns and planting apples and whatnot, all without government interference. But the obvious truth is such a life was short and miserable. Yes, we had a right to everything to which we joined our labor. Yes, our labor resulted in greater property, greater prosperity, and even the development of money, which enriched the provident and industrious.

And, yes, there was no government to tax it away from us.

But government isn't, of course, the only one that takes. While the industrious are busy working and gaining, the wicked are busy stealing. It is true that in the state of nature we each had an undisputed right to defend ourselves and our property. But good folks are often over-matched by the bad. So the obvious thing for ordinary people is to band together and find someone or construct some institutions that will protect them from the wicked and evil-intentioned. Thus it happens that, as our Declaration of Independence says, "governments are instituted among men" to protect us and our rights.

Note a few things. First, governments are "made." They are a product of human ingenuity resulting from human needs. Governments are human constructs. No one can say he's our "natural ruler." No one can say that God gave him a divine right to rule over us or over others. No one can say that he and his family "own" the country and all who live therein are his subjects. No one can say that the American colonies "belong" to Great Britain or that the American colonists are "subjects" of the British Crown.

While tyrannical government may be imposed on people, legitimate government is chosen by them. Indeed, it is only legitimate *if* they chose it. They may choose it passively, by agreeing to live under it, but it still is a choice. This is why the Declaration says that when a government no longer has the consent of the people, they have every right to change or abolish it.[50]

---

[50] "[T]o secure these rights, Governments are instituted among Men, deriving their just powers from the consent of the governed, — That whenever any Form of Government becomes destructive of these ends, it is the Right of the People to alter or to abolish it, and to institute new Government, laying its foundation on such principles and organizing its powers in such form, as to them shall seem most likely to effect their Safety and Happiness."

While everyone is born under one government or another, the people acting as a whole always have the collective right to change their government for one they think might suit them better.

The second thing to note is that governments are formed primarily for one purpose: to protect us. To protect our persons, to protect our property, and to protect our rights. There is, again, no reason to read this terribly narrowly, as some libertarians might. It is not only for national defense and to protect the obligation of contracts that men seek the protection of a government. We also always have, as the Declaration notes, the right to the "pursuit of happiness." We have a right to live our life to its fullest, to be all that our talents and luck and enterprise can help make us to be. And government exists to help secure this right as well as our other more concrete rights, rights such as life and property.

Put more broadly, it is, as Lincoln said, the proper role of government to help us do what we cannot do on our own or cannot do as well on our own.[51] So if we, as a democratic people, decide that we want help to combat cancer, or to establish post offices and post roads, or to build up the infrastructure of the nation, there is nothing illegitimate about such activities. We did not establish government to make our lives more difficult. We simply have to be careful that, in helping us in what we ask, the government not undermine the enjoyment of our rights, or work to change us from independent and self-reliant individuals to a dependent and entitlement-ridden people.

---

[51] "The legitimate object of government is to do for a community of people whatever they need to have done, but can not do *at all*, or can not do *so well do*, for themselves in their separate, and individual capacities." Lincoln, "Fragment on Government," 1854. Italics original.

In its broadest aspects, what most hinders our liberty and takes away from us our rights is power. Unrestrained political power can and always will undermine liberty. All political power needs to be balanced, limited, and watched. But despite loose talk from both ends of the political spectrum, government power isn't always the enemy of our liberty. Liberty can also be diminished by concentrated economic power, by powerful individuals who treat us as means towards their end, by mullahs and imams, by tribes and states, by customs and traditions that reject the doctrine of human equality, even by the awesome power of the natural world — fire, floods, plagues, disease, death.

Often power in one area has to be balanced or counteracted by power elsewhere. It was the power of vicious people who had designs on our property and our lives in the state of nature that impelled us to give government the authority to protect us in the first place. It was, in part, the power of foreign foes that impelled us to construct a strong and energetic Constitution and abandon the Articles of Confederation. The power of slaveholders over black men and women, who were born to freedom like everyone else, would not have been broken anytime soon except through the countervailing power of the federal government and the Union army. Governmental power is not always the enemy. Sometimes it's the solution. Or, as Alexander Hamilton says in the very first of *The Federalist Papers*, "the vigor of government is essential to the security of liberty."[52]

With this understanding of liberty and power, it should be possible for American conservatives to talk

---

[52] To cite Hamilton more fully: "An enlightened zeal for the energy and efficiency of government will be stigmatized [by those who are always critical of governmental power] as the offspring of a temper fond of despotic power and hostile to the preservation of liberty." Such people, it seems, have "forgotten that the vigor of government is essential to the security of liberty."

to American liberals over a broad range of issues. Think, for example, of the support across the spectrum for a government both active and energetic in keeping Americans secure from the workings of international terrorism. Conservatives and liberals may differ on how much and when governmental power is necessary, but we have shown that both sides can make common cause against commonly recognized enemies of human liberty.

True American conservatives are not anti-government "libertarians," nor are they close to anti-police, anti-CIA, anti-FBI, ACLU left-wing activists. Conservatives have to recognize that Hamilton had it right — In this dangerous world the vigor of government is often essential to the preservation of our freedoms.

So America begins with the notion — unheard of in human history — that the leading role of government is to protect us and to protect the exercise of our rights, that is, to protect our freedom. This is what would distinguish America from all previous nations. Even the ones that seemed most free — take Athens at its height — could never claim anything approaching the freedom we Americans would claim for ourselves.

* * * * *

In the Preamble to the Constitution, the Founding Fathers said that they wrote the Constitution in order to help us achieve six things: To form "a more perfect Union"; that is, to put aside the old Articles of Confederation and have a stronger, more unified country. Second, to establish justice. Third, to insure domestic tranquility; that is, to keep the peace throughout the new union and put down lawlessness. Fourth, to provide for the common defense. Fifth, to promote the general welfare — that is, the common good and not the good of this group or the interest of that class.

Writers often build up to the most important thing they wish to say, and perhaps that is the case with the Constitution. Everything that the Founders hoped to accomplish seems to culminate in the longest phrase of the Preamble, the sixth and final phrase: "to secure the Blessings of Liberty to ourselves and our Posterity."

Moreover, it is not just "Liberty" but "the Blessings of Liberty" that our Constitution will work to give us. "Blessings" is, of course, a religious word. I imagine some people might have thought it an odd word to use when talking about individuals following their own inclinations and looking to satisfy their deepest desires. It is true that we often think of the Founders as a rather dour group, perhaps a bit puritanical. But all of them, no matter how strongly or weakly religious they might have been, knew that their God wanted us to be happy, not only in heaven but also here in this mundane world. Freedom may have had a bad name in certain European religious circles — as it does today still in so many parts of the non-Western world, where submission to God's will, not the pursuit of our own individual happiness, is supposed to be the chief occupation of life. But the Founders saw no incompatibility between living our lives by the best of our lights and following God's will. It was both "Nature and Nature's God" that implanted in our hearts the desire to be free, and it was not blasphemous at all to act on that natural and God-given impulse.

But what exactly are these "blessings" of liberty? I think the Founders would have identified two: one to the individual and one to the whole society. To the individual, the blessings are almost obvious. First, not to be forced to worship gods you don't believe in.

Moreover, not to be forced to be what others want you to be; that is, for example, to pursue an occupation you find suited and satisfying. Or perhaps to devote your life to learning, or to making money, or to honor and reputation, or to God and prayer, or to service to others ... or to any combination of these goals and many others.

Of course, none of this comes with a "guarantee" of your happiness. But not being able to pursue your happiness as you see it would almost certainly result in misery. We have a hard enough time knowing how best to pursue our own happiness. Why would handing over those decisions to others — most especially to government — make our lives happier?

These connections between freedom and individual happiness seems almost intuitively obvious. But what's the connection between individual freedom and societal happiness? Most of the world seems to believe they are not connected at all — that the more individuals pursue their own interests, the more the rest of society suffers. Look at the history of collectivist societies: As they all believe, it is only through everyone being directed in what to do, everyone being fitted to good of the whole, that the common good will be achieved. Submerge your will into the general will; act not for yourself but for the whole. Only then will a good society be fully realized.

Nothing could have been more foreign to the Founders than ideas such as these. It wasn't that they had a simple "belief" in individual rights or some vague "hope" that freedom might contribute to the general welfare and the common good. They knew it did. They knew that businessmen and inventors and explorers and farmers, each pursuing their own individual interests, would cause a general increase in goods and services throughout the society. They knew that increased prosperity comes generally through individuals pursuing their own gain while protected by government. They also knew from the small experience the colonists had with collectivism in the first colonies that central direction meant not more general wealth but more general poverty.

Still, while we and the Founders know this, neither history nor much of the rest of the world shares this view. I've seen this for myself abroad, where people are aghast at the thought of allowing individuals to drill for oil or make a profit from the land or from the earth's natural resources. "Our natural resources belong to all of us," they say indignantly. "No one can own them for himself." Then they're frustrated at how few crops get raised or how little ore gets mined or oil gets pumped, and they're ashamed that they have to rely on free-world countries to help them out.

But beyond the realm of economics, how can it be that our liberty is a blessing not only for each of us individually but for all of us together as well? How could it ever be that a free people, all in pursuit of their own diverse interests, might rise to the level of securing what the Founders dared to call the "general welfare"? How shall we so construct a nation where liberty might not only be cherished by each of us but also might become a benefit for all? As we may guess, this hardly happens automatically. Looked at in that manner, we might begin to see something of the complicated, demanding task the Founders faced.

* * * * *

It must be said from the outset that when the Founders constructed a Constitution to secure our liberty, it wasn't a liberty in the small things of life — how I will dress today or whether I shall eat potatoes

for dinner — but a freedom in the most important ma-
ters of life.

In the centuries preceding our war for independence, thousands upon thousands of people in Europe
and elsewhere were killed over religion. Today, we
tend to think it outrageous that people would fight
over different opinions of religious dogma. But
whether a society followed or broke God's laws,
whether our neighbors taught our children false lessons and put them at risk of damnation, and whether
our country was pleasing to God were not considered
insignificant matters to our European ancestors. Worried about the judgment of God, good men and
women thought it right that proper orthodoxy and
obedience to God's will should be enforced by the
highest public authorities — enforced, if necessary, by
the stake and the sword.

So dissidents were persecuted in both the old world
and the new. The last person to be punished for denying the Trinity in the English-speaking world was
hanged in Scotland in 1698. Catholics had persecuted
Protestants in Europe, and Protestants returned the
favor both there and in the colonies. Even those who
came to the New World to avoid religious persecution
often did not hesitate to harass others who believed
differently. Nearly a century before our Independence,
Massachusetts was still publicly hanging Quakers.
And the Salem witch trials, which resulted in the
hanging or stoning of 20 men and women for sorcery,
took place barely 80 years before the Declaration of
Independence.

Today, millions of religious fanatics still populate
the globe. Around the world, people are being jailed
for blasphemy or murdered for heresy and apostasy. If
we dare say to these zealots that we, in the West, have
freedom of religion, that what a person might believe

is definitely a private and not public matter — well, their response is rarely one of admiration. What could be of greater importance than obeying God's will, saving our souls, and protecting the nation from divine wrath? Do you not see, they ask, how liberty for you in these matters might result in damnation for us all? Why shouldn't the full force of the community come down on those who would put a whole country on the path of destruction?

Yet in America, more than two centuries ago, Thomas Jefferson wrote a law that he later said was more important for America than all that he ever did as president, the Virginia Statute of Religious Freedom (1779):

> [N]o man shall be compelled to frequent or support any religious worship, place, or ministry whatsoever, nor shall be enforced, restrained, molested, or burthened in his body or goods, nor shall otherwise suffer, on account of his religious opinions or belief; but that all men shall be free to profess, and by argument to maintain, their opinions in matters of religion, and that the same shall in no wise diminish, enlarge, or affect their civil capacities.

This was a major intellectual step for mankind. Henceforward it would not be in small things where men and women would be free, but in some of the most serious and socially consequential aspects of life. How one worshipped, or even whether one worshipped at all, was now in the realm of freedom, not under the jurisdiction of compulsion. In a similar manner, how men and women raised their children, how industrious a person was, what social and political views one held, how openly one chose to express them, what one wrote, whom one decided to associate with — all these matters were now private matters, not public. Henceforward it would seem that not only private happiness but also the public good would be better served by leaving each man free to decide how he will live his life and how he will work and worship than by coercion.

But why would removing issues of free speech, press, association, and especially religion from the realm of politics have valued social consequences? Well, if peace is one of the great desiderata of life — "domestic tranquility," as the Constitution calls it — then freedom is one of the greatest means to that end. "Mind your own business" may sound like a sharp and unpleasant retort, but it's actually a foundational notion of societal harmony. Such freedom can help solve the problem of civil turmoil and war in much the same way that removing the question of economic justice — who deserves what and how much — from intrusive political control helped solve the problem of want and dismal poverty, as we saw in a previous chapter.

The more important the issues — how we should worship, how we should raise our children, what virtues we will or will not practice — the more men will dispute them, even to the point of the sword. So our Founders instructed us, and our experience tells us, to do the most counterintuitive thing: de-politicize these issues. Remove these matters from the realm of public control. Let government act when public force is truly necessary as in the protection of life, property, safety, security, and foreign defense. Let it act as well as in matters of social betterment where compromise is possible — rates of tariff, the building of roads, the extent of public "safety nets," the amount spent on scientific exploration or public education, and so on.

Seen in this way, our liberty is not only an end, a goal in and of itself, but also a means to other, greater, ends. While other nations might see freedom of religion as an offense to the demands of God, we Americans understand that religious freedom is one of the surest and clearest means to both individual happiness and societal peace. No longer will we be afraid that someone will behead us because we believe the wrong thing; no longer will we kill one another over matters of faith or ritual. Yes, I'm sure we can all catalogue the ways in which our society would be better if everyone went to church, prayed regularly and properly, and tried to live a holy life. But I'm equally sure we all recognize the clear, everyday benefits that come with not regulating religious views and not trying to establish "acceptable" religious practices.

The same is true with freedom of speech. Of course people will say hurtful things; lies will permeate the public press; gossip and un-neighborly backbiting will abound. But we still recognize that the widest allowance for free speech is consistently more a benefit than a liability in hundreds, even thousands of ways.

So, the Constitution's Preamble has it exactly right. It's not only liberty in itself that we honor, but the "Blessings of Liberty," that is, all the good that liberty brings us: greater domestic tranquility, new avenues to the truth, greater prosperity, and a better chance at happiness for each of us.

* * * * *

Still, no matter how carefully we try to delineate the good consequences of liberty and the virtues of a nation founded on the protection of individual rights, the practice of liberty is not without its problems. Even we, who live and prosper under our regime of liberty, have concerns, and it's probably good to put our concerns out on the table.

Often there's a sense that liberty has been taken too far; that we have become not a rights-respecting society but a rights-saturated society: a society where "rights" stand in direct opposition to morality, public decency, and personal responsibility. For example, not all Americans are proud of abortion on demand, sex and graphic violence on every media outlet, the easy dissolution of family ties, and the odiousness of so much of what passes for contemporary "culture."

Everywhere we turn we see our fellow citizens claiming a right to use foul or obscene language anywhere they choose. Everywhere we hear that freedom of speech means freedom of "expression" — any and all expression.

Is it a good or a bad thing that we seem to have expanded our list of "rights" far beyond our most basic and historic rights so that they now include every thing our hearts and imaginations might desire? Is a nation truly devoted as America is to individual rights and to securing the "Blessings of Liberty" incapable of ever saying "No" to anything except at the furthest margins — and sometimes not even then?

Because we seem confused about rights — that is, confused about the cornerstone of our constitutional republic, and because our defense of rights in their most extreme manifestations has caused many in the world to question the very value of liberal democratic life, let us delve even deeper into what the Founders understood on this most crucial matter.

The Constitution and its Bill of Rights list a few basic rights. But the list is not exhaustive,[53] nor does either of those documents ever specify the full meaning of the rights they set out. And other than saying that our true rights ultimately stem from an understanding of Nature (and, thus, from a proper understanding of what is appropriate for man as man), the Declaration

---

[53] "The enumeration in the Constitution, of certain rights, shall not be construed to deny or disparage others retained by the people." Amendment IX.

doesn't pretend to give an exhaustive explanation of what all our rights might be. It simply notes that we have certain unalienable rights and that "among these" are "life, liberty and the pursuit of happiness."

In order to get to this question of the meaning and scope of our rights, let us begin by stating a principle that may seem wrong on first sight, though it is actually incontrovertible: No matter what part of the political spectrum you see yourself as on, you are wrong to believe that your favorite rights are absolute. Yes, they may be important, central, even vital, to a good, just, and prosperous polity; they may help you satisfy your highest hopes, make you wealthier, give you peace — but they are not absolute. To believe that rights highlighted by liberals — such as speech and press and "expression" — are unlimited cannot be true. A free people can still have laws against perjury or libel or misrepresenting what you sell. The same is true of conservatives championing the right to property or to bear arms. Even the most sacred and central of our rights — perhaps the right to the free exercise of religion or the right to defend ourselves against potential harm — has limits, even obvious limits.

But why are rights limited? Even though we rightly profess a belief in near total freedom of religion, no sane society would let fathers sacrifice their children for religion's sake or allow a husband to have his living wife buried with him upon his death, even with her loving consent. We rightly have trouble with arguments that parents can deny medical care to their children because they have faith in God's providence. While we correctly say that we want as much freedom of speech as possible, we also correctly say that no one has the right falsely to yell fire in a crowded theatre, or argue politics through a bullhorn in a residential neighborhood at 2 in the morning. Even the most ardent supporter of the Second Amendment has to admit that the right to bear arms cannot include the right to carry bazookas on the street or own small nuclear weapons. The right to travel can legitimately be abridged by your local Board of Health quarantining individuals with dread diseases. And reasonable people admit that, while the right to private ownership is a bedrock right of our society, we still understand that property can be regulated in many ways, from taxation to zoning to eminent domain.

So, when it comes to rights, the one absolute is that no right is ever absolute.

But what is it, exactly, that bounds our right? What is it that declares what is a right and what isn't? Moreover, who is to say? Who referees those boundaries or says when we have taken our rights "too far"? Indeed, who is to say when something is even a "right" at all?

In the next chapter we'll try to give some answers to the question, Who is the referee? But for now let's consider what bounds our rights, even rights such as freedom of speech and religion and press. Perhaps, in doing so, we may get greater clarity on what makes something a "right" in the first place.

We all seem comfortable with recognizing that our rights are limited by the rights of others. As the saying goes, your right to swing your fist ends at the tip of my nose. Your right to promote your candidate in a residential neighborhood through a bullhorn at night is restricted by the rights of me and my neighbors to sleep in peace.

Those seem like easy questions with easy answers. Yes, your right not to be libeled restrains my freedom of speech and press. But does your desire not to hear foul speech on the subway or your desire not to witness what you perceive of as lewd conduct trump my right to free expression? Does a community really have the "right" to ban porn shops, establish curfew hours, prevent prostitution, establish a draft, or keep your DNA on file?

I think the answer is yes, though dangers and difficulties must be recognized. Perhaps the first way of approaching this problem is by understanding that "individual rights" may not be the only kinds of rights there are. Sure, the rights to life, liberty, and the pursuit of happiness reside in each one of us equally and individually. Nevertheless, "libertarians" on the right and those on the ACLU left often have difficulty recognizing that sometimes "We" and not just "I" have rights. But, as we noted before, the Declaration had no trouble in talking about something Jefferson called rights "of the People" — everything from the right to change our form of government to the right to secure our collective "Safety and Happiness."[54]

Thus, the Founders would have no difficulty recognizing that while the accused have a right to a fair trial with due process, the rest of us have a right to public safety free of burdensome rules on police investigations or overly difficult roadblocks to evidence gathering. Similarly, our right to public peace sometimes limits the speech rights of the loud and aggressive, even when they're talking politics or religion — the type of speech the First Amendment is most interested in protecting. And parents are entitled, as a group, to raise their children without the bombardment of public displays of vulgarity, lasciviousness, or violence. Simply put, two or more people do not have fewer rights than one.

---

[54] Again: "whenever any Form of Government becomes destructive of these ends, it is the Right of the People to alter or to abolish it, and to institute new Government, laying its foundation on such principles and organizing its powers in such form, as to them shall seem most likely to effect their Safety and Happiness."

Why is it that when we talk about the idea that we, the people, have rights, some assume that we've thereby subtracted from the sum of Americans' rights, or that rights have now been "abrogated"? To recognize, support, and make effective our rights as a people is not to diminish a free society but to buttress it. To deny felons or the mentally ill the right to carry arms increases the liberty of all, it does not reduce it. To deny the right of individuals to lie on the stand or publish libel adds to the freedoms we all enjoy. To help parents keep pornography or drugs out of their neighborhoods increases the freedom of parents to raise their children as they deem necessary. And all of these are rights, to use the language of the Declaration, that we have never alienated.

Will sometimes the rights of "We" overreach? Will they sometimes intrude too far into what should be the domain of individual freedoms? Yes, of course — just as the rights of individuals have often and repeatedly reached too far the other way.

For example, it would have been inconceivable to the Founders — as it seems also inconceivable to common sense — that "free speech" with near absolute First Amendment protection would include video games depicting, as well as giving children the ability to participate in, simulated rapes, eviscerations, and disembowelments, with "points" for torturing mothers and raping their daughters or for exterminating racial or ethnic groups. Yet, sadly, that's exactly how the Court recently ruled, with an opinion written by an often quite libertarian justice and happily joined by the more liberal-left members of the Court.[55]

Cherishing liberty and cultivating the "Blessings of Liberty" does not mean, cannot mean, and has never

---

[55] *Brown v. Entertainment Merchants Association,* 131 S. Ct. 2729 (2011). The majority opinion was by Justice Scalia.

meant, simply giving liberty free reign in all matters. I understand the fear we all have in opening the door to tyranny in any of its forms. But the problem with both the far left and the libertarian right is that their often unbounded view of rights is not only destructive of other goods *but of liberty itself*. In this regard, we all should take very seriously the warning made by James Madison at the end of *Federalist*, No. 63: "that liberty may be endangered by the abuses of liberty, as well as by the abuses of power; that there are numerous instances of the former as well as of the latter; and that the former rather than the latter is apparently most to be apprehended by the United States."

The idea that that our freedoms are all at risk if everyone can do whatever he or she desires in the name of liberty — and that these abuses of liberty are a greater threat to our country than the abuses of power — should be first shocking, then sobering. If, in the name of "rights," anyone can peddle violent and degrading videos, or the deranged can carry arms, or our criminal justice system is hostage to the accused, or if every interest and desire automatically becomes clothed with the mantle of a "right," then "rights" and "liberty" chance becoming terms not of admiration and respect but of contempt. And with that, Liberty, with all its Blessings, will run the risk of being lost.

- V -

Establishing America's Constitutional Democracy

THE FOUNDERS GAVE US a nation founded on two basic principles: control of government by the people, and the desire to protect the enjoyment of our natural rights. But these two objectives do not always or easily go together. And when we try to incorporate the other desiderata the Founders mention in the Preamble — justice and promoting the general welfare, domestic tranquility, national defense — well, the problems seem to mount.[56]

Let's begin by taking seriously the matter of combining rights with democratic rule. Let's ask a serious and critical question: How can it be that a Constitution meant to "secure the Blessings of Liberty" was written without a Bill of Rights? To Madison, the violation of rights by the various newly independent states led "more than anything," to the writing of the new Constitution.[57] But without a Bill of Rights, how serious were the Founders about the security of liberty? How do we know that their statements honoring liberty weren't more than simply fine words or, worse, a cover for securing their own private interests?

This lack of anything like a Bill of Rights was raised by the Anti-Federalists and seems to have taken the writers of the Constitution by surprise. The Anti-

---

[56] Again, the Preamble reads, "We the People of the United States, in Order to form a more perfect Union, establish Justice, insure domestic Tranquility, provide for the common defense, promote the general Welfare, and secure the Blessings of Liberty to ourselves and our Posterity, do ordain and establish this CONSTITUTION for the United States of America."

[57] Farrand, op. cit., Volume I, p. 134.

Federalists claimed this was a mortal defect, and they threatened to oppose ratifying the Constitution unless a genuine Bill of Rights was added.

The writers of the Constitution took this threat seriously and so, under Madison's leadership, the first Congress proposed a list of 12 amendments. Ten of these were soon adopted by the requisite number of states, and they were appended to the Constitution as what we now always call "the Bill of Rights."

But why were the Founders originally against a Bill of Rights? After all, if the document were truly meant to protect liberty as the Preamble promises, why not just lay out our rights out and not leave anything to chance?

One response the Founders gave was correct, but perhaps not totally convincing: How could we ever write down all the rights we the people have? Do people have a right to wear a hat if they so choose? Well, of course. So, should we write a constitution that says people have a right to wear or not wear a hat? Or how about the right to go fishing, or to hunt, or to whistle while they worked? You see, once we start laying out our rights, there's no end to all the things we'll have to list.[58]

But this line of reasoning led to another more serious argument: Writing a Bill of Rights is risky since, if we leave out a particular right, the government might think such a right wasn't protected, and the door would be open for the government to move against that right or curtail it. Does a farmer have a right freely to eat what he grows on his own land? In a case that's still on the books, the Supreme Court has held, "No, he doesn't."[59]

---

[58] See 1 Annals of Congress, Gales and Seaton, eds., 1834, especially pp. 759-60.

[59] *Wickard v. Filburn* 317 U.S. 111 (1942).

In the end, the writers of the Constitution gave in and proposed the Bill of Rights that we currently have. Of course, little in life is ever an unalloyed good. I imagine the Anti-Federalists would be aghast to see how what they proposed in order to restrain political power has transmogrified itself into a handy vehicle for judicial supremacy and the breakdown of federalism. Nevertheless, its proposal by Madison did secure the final ratification of the Constitution, and it serves to remind us that we are indeed a nation built on the protection of rights and that the "Blessings of Liberty" truly are central to our way of life.

However, there was one more instructive argument against listing our rights. We have not seen fit to include a Bill of Rights in the Constitution, Hamilton said in one of *The Federalist Papers*, because *the Constitution itself fits that purpose even without a Bill of Rights*: "[T]he Constitution is itself, in every rational sense, and to every useful purpose, A BILL OF RIGHTS."[60]

How so? How is it that Hamilton could claim that the original Constitution as it came out of Philadelphia in 1787, before the drafting of the Bill of Rights, was in its very essence and "to every useful purpose" itself a Bill of Rights?

Well, the federal government is, first of all, limited. It is not a government, Hamilton says, capable of reaching matters of "personal or private concern" (as the state governments certainly could), but only had under its purview "the general political interests of the nation."[61] The thought that the federal government might someday claim for itself the power to regulate individual health-care plans or own a controlling in-

---

[60] *Federalist*, No. 84.

[61] Ibid.

terest in a major American industry, or attempt to direct the curricula of local schools, for example, would have been unthinkable to the Founders.

But this is not to say that the federal government was given only minor tasks to perform. Within its sphere, the central or federal government has amazing strength. It, and it alone, can declare war and commit the entire nation to battle. No state can do that even though we still sometimes refer to them as "sovereign" states. Only the federal government can make treaties with foreign nations, and those treaties are binding throughout the nation. Only the federal government can coin money. No longer can popular majorities in the states try to defraud creditors by printing paper money and so inflate the currency that all debts become worthless. The federal government can tax, can regulate interstate and foreign commerce, and can raise and support national armed forces.[62]

Just as crucial, the Constitution limited the activity of the federal government to certain highly important, even the most important, national political matters — and at the same time kept the government from intruding in both private matters and local matters where it would have neither ability nor competence. We didn't need a Bill of Rights to tell us that Congress can't establish an official church or shut down the local newspaper. Those powers were never given to it.

"But," some might say, "what about the 'necessary and proper' clause, which seems to give the government the power to do whatever it thinks necessary and proper — isn't that a gift of unlimited power?" Well, no, not at all, though we all know that some people think it is. All that the "necessary and proper" clause says is that the federal government has the

---

[62] See Article I, section 8 of the Constitution, in the appendix to this book.

power "to make all laws which shall be necessary and proper for carrying into execution the forgoing [listed] powers, and all other powers vested by this Constitution in the government of the United States, or in any department or officer thereof."

What this means is not that there's a wide-ranging grant of power for Congress to pass whatever laws it thinks might be "necessary" or "proper," but only those additional laws needed *to carry out the powers already listed.*

Look at it this way: The power of the Federal government to punish those who rob the mail is not enumerated anywhere in the Constitution. But the power "to establish post offices and post roads" is listed. Might it be "necessary and proper" for the government to have the authority to punish a person who robs a post office or who steals from your mailbox, as a necessary and proper part of its establishment of a postal system? Sure. Or does Congress have the authority to build a fence along our border with Mexico, or have the border patrolled by federal agents? Of course it has that power — though nowhere in the Constitution is "the power to build a fence along the Mexican border" listed. But such authority is both proper and necessary to carry out the listed powers of the federal government to provide for the common defense and to regulate the naturalization of aliens. That's really all the "necessary and proper" phrase means.

Moreover, far from being a grant of power to Congress, the phrase is in a real sense a limitation on federal power since it clearly says not that Congress can do whatever it wants to carry out its powers, but only that it can do those things that are both necessary and proper.

But let us return to the idea that the Founders wrote for us a Constitution that, in itself, was the equivalent of a Bill of Rights — indeed, far better than a simple listing of rights on parchment.

Besides the fact that the Constitution establishes a limited national government, with formidable but still circumscribed authority, the next and most obvious thing is that what we have is a *written* constitution. What other major nation in 1787 had a written constitution? Not France, not Great Britain. Not, for that matter, any other country. Only the newly freed American states had written constitutions, and it was in part the success of those documents that showed us the importance of such a document.

But what, exactly, is its importance? The very fact that the Constitution is written is without doubt the first and greatest limitation on arbitrary power that there is. We alone of all the great nations of the world had a document that set down in print what was allowed and what was forbidden. We alone set out how our legislators and presidents were to be elected, how long they could serve and under what conditions, and what their authority would be. Even in the middle of a great Civil War and two world wars, the Constitution set out when the commander-in-chief had to stand for election. No one, not Lincoln, not FDR, could say that the time for re-election was inopportune, that the voting for president had to be postponed. No Congress can say that it wishes to go beyond its mandate and, for example, strip the states of their power to set up local schools or build whatever roads they might think necessary. No Congress can deny a President his veto power or his right to nominate cabinet officers and govern the executive branch.

To be sure, all of us can name a dozen instances where we are certain the Constitution has been violated by Congress or the President or the Court.[63] But so long as we have a written constitution, we the people have the most potent means of changing direction and righting the wrong. We have the supreme law of the land set down in concrete form that we can rally to.

This is, in part, why constant recourse to the Constitution is so important; why an understanding of the Constitution by the people in general and not just by lawyers or judges is so important; why teaching the Constitution in the schools is so important; and why respect, even reverence, for the document is so important. We could have established a government without ever writing a Constitution to govern it. Or we could have written a document that only philosophers and judges could understand. But we didn't do any of that. "We the People" ordained and established a Constitution in clear written form for us to read, to understand, and to apply. No other government before us, and precious few after us, can say that.

But things written on paper are only (as the Founders might say) "parchment barriers." We needed more than words; *we needed strong and viable institutions.* We needed to grant sufficient power to the government to protect us and promote the nation's wellbeing, yet we had to have *serious and substantive ways of controlling the use of that power.*

Because the federal government was not given puny or weak powers by the Constitution, it was absolutely necessary for the Founders to find ways of controlling the exercise of those powers. The power to tax, to declare war, to make peace, to raise armies, to regulate interstate commerce, to coin money, even to

---

[63] Yes, even the Supreme Court can violate — or, if you prefer, "misread" and "misapply" — the Constitution. Indeed, every time the Court overturns its own decisions, it's saying that it now knows it was wrong in what it previously did.

suppress insurrections that might arise within a state — coupled with the power to do all that might be necessary and proper in their execution — these powers are hardly insignificant. Indeed, these are great and fearsome powers, the full power of national sovereignty.

And because these powers are so formidable, it was incumbent on Madison and others to find ways both *external* to the government and *within the government itself* to restrain the illegitimate use of these powers and thus help protect freedom. Or, to refer to Madison directly: "In framing a government which is to be administered by men over men, the great difficulty lies in this: you must first enable the government to control the governed; and in the next place oblige it to control itself."[64]

The primary means of controlling our government "externally" is by means of regular set elections. But the means the Founders devised for having the government *hold itself* in check are all those ever-so-boring items we learned way back in civics class: bicameralism, separation of powers, checks and balances, and the rest. The trouble is, while they might seem boring, they are absolutely vital for the success of free and rational democratic governance.

* * * * *

To get a clearer picture of how the Constitution itself, without a Bill of Rights, is the greatest protector of our liberties, let's look at Congress. The first obvious thing is that Congress isn't an "it" but a "they": A House of Representatives and a Senate. But why? Wouldn't one compact legislative body be both more democratic and more efficient? Yes, but let's not for-

---

[64] *Federalist*, No. 51. "Oblige it" in this sense means to force or compel it.

get that *better* democracy, not "more" democracy, was the aim of the Founders. And, yes, a single body would be more "efficient." And that's exactly the reason the Founders didn't establish it!

"In republican government" Madison tells us in *Federalist*, No. 51, "the legislative authority, necessarily, predominates." It is Congress that makes the laws that govern the country. So what might be done to keep tabs on Congress and help assure that the legislation it passes is responsible and conducive to liberty? "The remedy," Madison tells us, is "to divide the legislature into different branches; and to render them by different modes of election, and different principles of action, as little connected with each other, as the nature of their common functions, and their common dependence on the society, will admit."[65]

Requiring two branches of the legislature to agree before any law can be passed, with each elected in different ways, from different constituencies and for different lengths of time, increases the probability that *what they both agree on will be broadly acceptable and not factional, more thoughtful and deliberate, and less likely to be subversive of the rights of this or that group.*

One house (the House of Representatives) would be elected by the people in relatively small districts directly by the voters. The other (the Senate) would be a smaller and more deliberative body chosen by states (not small districts) and whose members had longer terms and a higher age qualification. This arrangement gave the first branch the character of direct sympathy with the feelings of the people and the second branch the character of greater stability, greater

---

[65] *Federalist*, No. 51.

freedom to deliberate, and fewer fears that some momentary passion or excitement in the electorate will suddenly sweep them from office.[66]

We Americans often complain — we have always complained — that Congress is slow and cumbersome, prone to inaction and even deadlock. But the Founders clearly were more comfortable with that outcome than with the chaos, confusion, and injustice characteristic of the wild democratic regimes of the past.

* * * * *

"Bicameralism" — as we all learned to call it in high school — is one of the many *institutional arrangements* the Founders established to break up concentrations of political power, retard governmental activity, and use one part of the government to watch over and check the other parts — all for the sake of protecting liberty without the artificiality of a "Bill of Rights." It was through this and similar constitutional arrangements that the Founders hoped to moderate and restrain democratic rule while still holding true to the character of popular government.

All the different structures and institutions of our government — bicameralism, separation of powers, checks and balances, judicial review, calendared elections, the electoral college, the various terms of office — were meant to refine and moderate our democracy in the same way. They were designed to slow down legislation, hopefully infuse greater deliberation into the process, restrain unwarranted political power,

---

[66] Of course this means that we fool ourselves if we think that "gridlock" in Washington is something new or out of the ordinary or signals a "breakdown" of our democratic system. The system was purposefully designed so that bills and nominations that have wide support across the country will have easier sailing than controversial or highly partisan proposals will ever have. There is nothing "unconstitutional" about gridlock — indeed, the only thing unconstitutional about it is when a President thinks a gridlock gives him the power to act on his own.

and, in the end, help ensure the preservation of liberty. It is, in this way, that Hamilton could legitimately say that the Constitution was "in every rational sense and for every practical purpose" itself a Bill of Rights.[67]

* * * * *

Before our Constitution, all previous democracies (including the democracies in the 13 newly freed American states) were prone to make not only passionate, even chaotic, decisions but, worse, unjust and illiberal decisions. The Founders gave us a complex, redundant structure that tried to force compromise, moderation, and repeated second looks.

But their genius was deeper than this. Oddly, these days we tend to overlook something the Founders insisted on that was even more central to the preservation of our freedom — American pluralism.

Before 1787, almost every philosopher and politician who wanted to make democracy work talked about the need to build *unity* among the people. If all citizens would just be of one class, or of one religious persuasion, or of one mind on the most important things, democracies would be more harmonious and peaceful. We even hear it these days — it's only the tiniest "one percent" that denies us all economic justice; enforce greater equality for all, bring us all together as one, and our country will finally become fair and just. Differences among the people mean strife and civil war; but equality and unity mean peace, fair-

---

[67] Does it always work? No, not always. Sometimes, the retardant and protective benefit of bicameralism and separation of powers can be overcome when both houses of Congress are controlled by one party and the president is of the same party. Then the awkwardness of protective gridlock can be replaced by improper and unwarranted partisanship and the silencing of cross-party accommodation. The passage of the Patient Protection and Affordable Care Act of 2010 ("Obamacare") is clearly the most recent example of this.

ness, and just democratic rule. This is why most people who thought about democracy before Madison thought democracy worked best in small, homogenous city-states where people could be unified in class, religion, occupation, and outlook.

But Madison looked at the 13 small, newly freed states and saw in them not harmony and respect for rights but the opposite. Democracy in the states sometimes meant majorities trampling on the legitimate rights of minorities and individuals. Even in the smallest states, injustice seemed to be everywhere. (It was observed that in tiny Rhode Island, when debtors had control of the legislature, they so inflated the currency with legalized paper money that creditors took to hiding rather than be "paid back" with worthless scrip.)

Besides, Madison observed, to try to give all the people similar habits, similar passions and goals in life, or, even perhaps above all, similar economic status, would so trample on individual liberty that no democracy, no form of government, was worth it.

Madison also observed that rights seemed better protected in large and diverse places than in smaller places. Virginia and Pennsylvania seemed more "liberal" in the older and truer sense — that is, more protective of everyone's rights — than tiny Rhode Island or small theocratic Connecticut, where the Congregational Church was established as the official religion until 1818. Why? Simply because larger places have a diversity of different interests, outlooks, occupations, religions, families, and ethnicities. That is, individual and minority rights are more secure in a democracy where everyone is part of a minority group and where no religion or tribe or trade or occupation is, by itself, a majority.

"Extend the sphere," Madison tells us, "and you take in a greater variety of parties and interests." In so doing, "you make it less probable that a majority of the whole will have a common motive to invade the rights of other citizens...."[68] For instance, think about Northern Ireland, where so much seems to be a conflict between Catholics and Protestants; or Iraq, divided between Shi'a and Sunni; or the old American West, with its fights between ranchers and farmers. Whenever society is divided in two, divided between antagonistic groups who believe that the other group's gain is always at their expense, then a democracy that tries to protect the rights of all will rarely work. "Extend the sphere" — increase the country in size and take in literally hundreds of religions, occupations, nationalities — and everyone's rights will be better protected from abuse.

Or, to put it differently, make every interest group a *minority* interest group, incapable of controlling the government on its own. Make it so that each minority can only, in the end, pass legislation by listening to others, finding common ground, and moderating their demands. Then and only then will legislative majorities be made more moderate and less extreme, more inclusive and less single-minded, more expansive and less fanatical. It will still be a majority, but it will now be, Madison hoped, a compromised and more wide-ranging majority. And it will be a shifting, not permanent, majority, depending on the issues.

It will still be majority rule, for these now more moderated and inclusive majorities will generally predominate — but you will have warded off the worst of democratic despotism while still working within the boundaries of democratic governing. And even these

---

[68] *Federalist*, No. 10.

newly formed and broader majorities — let's say in the House of Representatives — are still subject to all we mentioned before: to senatorial review, presidential veto, and judicial oversight. Again, the Founders made it so that the brakes on precipitous and potentially intolerant actions are many and powerful.

Some students (and many professors) of American politics get it completely backwards when they read *Federalist*, No. 10, where Madison wrote about pluralism. They think that Madison is trying to strengthen factions, trying to empower special interest groups, trying to turn the country into the clash of powerful lobbies each vying to take power from the other. But just the opposite is true: Madison wanted to multiply the number of interests and groups and associations and trades so as to *weaken* the political power of any one of them. Once weakened, they could generally only succeed in Congress by moderating their individual demands, by finding areas of common agreement, and by compromising.

For example, clearly where there is no "majority " religious sect, religious liberty grows more secure. And so, Madison builds on this example:

> In a free government the security for civil rights must be the same as for religious rights. It consists in the one case in the multiplicity of interests, and in the other in the multiplicity of sects. The degree of security in both cases will depend on the number of interests and sects; and this may be presumed to depend on the extent of country and number of people comprehended under the same government.[69]

Notice that Madison does *not* say that the security for our civil rights in America lies in putting language

---

[69] Madison, *Federalist*, No. 51.

into a Bill of Rights in hopes that words will protect our religious and civil liberties. Nor does he want us to rely on something like the Supreme Court or any other single institution for our protection. Rather, it is the "multiplicity of interests" *working within a complex democratic framework* that will restrain our politics and help keep one group from invading the legitimate rights of another.

Enlarging the sphere, Madison noted, is "the only defense against the inconveniencies of democracy consistent with the democratic form of government."[70] Or, as Madison proudly says elsewhere, "in *the extent and proper structure* of the Union, therefore, we behold a republican remedy for the diseases most incident to republican government."[71]

Still, despite all that Madison and the other Founders tried to do to build up American pluralism in support of the protection of rights, there was one area where they glaringly and tragically failed: slavery. No matter how fast we expanded territorially, no matter how economically diverse we became, there was always the deep and irreconcilable division of the nation between free states and slave states. Over this issue we became, in effect, not a diverse nation but a divided nation. This simple division was so powerful and intense that it brushed aside all other interests and outlooks. Sadly, Madison was right: As history has always shown, a democracy divided in two will find it nearly impossible to avoid conflict, strife, and even civil war.

---

[70] Madison, Speech of June 6, in Farrand, *Records* I, pp. 134-35.

[71] *Federalist*, No. 10. Emphasis added.

* * * * *

Before we leave our discussion of the structure of government we inherited from the Founders, it's necessary to look at one more thing: American Federalism.

We have a tendency in recent times to compress this grand principle of government to narrow discussions of "states' rights" or "the Tenth Amendment." But we shouldn't lose sight of the greater picture first: While larger countries with a multiplicity of interests and groups are better for liberty and for purposes of defense and commerce, states exist because they are the best way for people to govern themselves in matters appropriate to themselves and their localities.

While we have what looks to all the world like some kind of mad political frenzy every four years over who will be the next president and give the country its direction, the real and ordinary governing of America takes place much more quietly, everyday, at our state and local levels. We truly learn how to govern ourselves in our states, cities and towns. We have to figure out, locally, how to shape our criminal and civil justice system in ways that make sense to our needs. We have to argue over housing ordinances and traffic speeds and water treatment plants and school bonds. We have to set up hospitals and hire teachers and punish robbers. We have to do a million things that teach us how to live with each other and to govern ourselves.

If everything were decided for us nationally — no matter how moderate and fair the central government might turn out to be — we would be no better off than when we were governed by the British crown. In a democracy, the more people can work together, hear each other out, compromise their differences, and actively solve their own problems, the finer is our democracy.

So the real benefit of Federalism is not that the states are "laboratories" of innovation, as we hear so often these days. They are, but only secondarily. Nor are they are the great protectors of our inalienable rights. Their main use and virtue is that they help make democracy real for all of us.

But we shouldn't jump from a philosophical defense of Federalism as the ground of democratic governing to a legalistic defense of "states' rights." Historically, little has done more harm to the cause of decent and thoughtful American conservatism than the doctrine of states' rights back when that looked to all the world as little more than a cover for racism.

If American conservatives are defenders of the idea of checked and limited government, then they will have to be very careful in their praise of the "rights" of states and localities, which often have a tendency to concentrate power in their political officials. The objects they govern may seem, in the grander scheme of things, small — schools, roads, local crimes, property rights — but petty tyrannies close at hand are hardly better than grand despotisms far away.

The Tenth Amendment was very careful not to say that states have "rights" — only people can have rights — but certain "powers": They retain those powers that have not been delegated to the federal government or prohibited to them by the Constitution. "The powers not delegated to the United States by the Constitution, nor prohibited by it to the States, are reserved to the States respectively, or to the people."

The truth is that our rights and liberties are often less secure locally than they are nationally. Jim Crow laws were always a state phenomenon, not national legislation. More violations and more serious violations of the right to property have been done locally than ever could be enacted nationally. (Although any number of instances could be cited, think only back to the recent case of *Kelo v. New London*, where the city of New London, Connecticut, took the private property of homeowners and gave it to private developers. Although a good bit of public fury was directed against the Supreme Court for its decision, it was the locality that itself committed the offense. The Court was simply upholding the principle of federalism in not overruling the city.)

Many of the Founders, with James Madison in the lead, were quick to point out that the reason for writing a new Constitution wasn't simply to better defend the nation or increase commerce, but to put an end to some of the more illiberal laws in the states. The Constitution as it came from the Convention and was first ratified had a long list of things that states might no longer do — everything from a prohibition on coining money to writing ex post facto laws to impairing the obligation of contracts.[72] The list of what states may *not* do was almost as long as the list of things the new central government *could* do.[73]

So, while Federalism is absolutely part of the grand design of the Constitution, too narrow an allegiance to "states' rights" or a simple reading of the Tenth Amendment will too easily put us on the side of less liberty and more government, sometimes of the most petty and destructive kind. Today, conservatives are called upon to be supporters of liberty and private and

---

[72] Madison was willing to go even further. In proposing the new Bill of Rights, he was hoping to have some of its most important provisions apply against the states as well as the federal government. Freedom of conscience and of the press and the right to trial by jury were all listed by Madison as rights that should be firmly protected from state action. Yet since the impetus for the Bill of Rights was to have further safeguards against *national* autocracy, the project was dropped.

[73] See Article I, section 10 of the Constitution in the Appendix to this book.

public right, defenders of the best of our traditions, and partisans of the philosophy of the Founders. They are not called upon to be apologists for state power.

* * x * *

The thrust of this chapter has been so far to present all the many ways in which the Founders' Constitution has been instrumental in securing, promoting, and protecting our rights both as individuals and as a people. But — let's be up front about it — there are many in America who chafe at the inefficiencies inherent in our constitutional arrangements, many with a different view of rights than the Founders' view, and even more with a different view of equality than our Founders. And, while one can see their positions and read their arguments in a myriad of political books and journals, unfortunately the sharpest way of attacking the work of the Founders these days seems to be to attack their character. If the Founders can be painted as against the common man, sexist, probably homophobic, and certainly racist, then the transformation of the country along more "modern," or more left-wing, lines can more easily happen.

These attempts to discredit the Founders and their Constitution has so entered the culture that we seem to hear it from everyone, from grade school teachers to university professors to Supreme Court Justices: The Founders were a bunch of racist white males who wrote a document that not only perpetuated their power but the power of their race. Indeed, so racist were our forefathers that they couldn't even see blacks as whole people, but only as three-fifths of a human.[74]

---

[74] See Justice Thurgood Marshall's "Bicentennial Speech" of May 6, 1987. This speech is remarkable not only for its historical obtuseness, but for Marshall's deprecation of the very document that gives him his judicial independence, a document which he took an oath to uphold.

To be sure, it would be wrong to pretend that the contradiction between slavery and freedom is a small matter. And, yes, there were surely those some in 1776 and 1787 who wanted to cover up the Jeffersonian idea of the equality of all men or make the idea of freedom apply only to themselves. Nonetheless, both the Declaration of Independence and the Constitution still pointed to the equal liberty of all, even when that liberty it couldn't be immediately implemented and even when it went against the real interests of so many of the Founders themselves.

It is indisputable that there were some delegates to the Constitutional Convention who owned slaves — including Washington and Madison. Was it wrong for them to own slaves? Of course it was — no man may justly "own" another human. Did those Founders who owned slaves know it was wrong? Yes, they did. So how should we understand this seemingly glaring contradiction? And how far does this contradiction taint the work they produced?

Jefferson, himself a slaveholder, tried in 1776 to make the Declaration of Independence an even stronger anti-slavery document, but that the delegates from a few of the southern colonies refused to sign it as Jefferson wrote it. He wanted the document to condemn the slave trade, and George III's support of it, in the strongest terms possible. The full paragraph Jefferson wrote was:

> [H]e has waged cruel war against human nature itself, violating it's most sacred rights of life & liberty in the persons of a distant people who never offended him, captivating & carrying them into slavery in another hemisphere, or to incur miserable death in their transportation thither. This piratical warfare, the opprobrium of *infidel* powers, is the warfare of the CHRISTIAN king of Great Britain. Determined

to keep open a market where MEN should be bought & sold, he has prostituted his negative for suppressing every legislative attempt to prohibit or to restrain this execrable commerce: and that this assemblage of horrors might want no fact of distinguished die, he is now exciting those very people to rise in arms among us, and to purchase that liberty of which *he* has deprived them, by murdering the people upon whom *he* also obtruded them; thus paying off former crimes committed against the *liberties* of one people, with crimes which he urges them to commit against the *lives* of another.

Note that Jefferson wrote the word "MEN" as it appears here so as to underscore the possession of natural rights, including the right to live free, by everyone, not just whites or Englishmen. Jefferson never once in anything he wrote justified slavery or saw those who were enslaved as anything less than fully human and unjustly treated.

But Jefferson's Declaration had to settle for the simple but still fully radical proclamation that all men — blacks included — had an inalienable right to liberty, even if their freedom couldn't be made manifest immediately. No doubt Abraham Lincoln said it best:

They [the signers of the Declaration] defined with tolerable distinctness, in what respects they did consider all men created equal — equal in 'certain inalienable rights, among which are life, liberty, and the pursuit of happiness.' This they said, and this meant. They did not mean to assert the obvious untruth, that all were then actually enjoying that equality, nor yet, that they were about to confer it immediately upon them. In fact they had no power to confer such a boon. They meant simply to declare the right, so that the enforcement of it might follow as fast as circumstances should permit. They meant to set up a standard maxim for free society, which should be familiar to all, and revered by all; constantly looked to, constantly labored for, and even though never perfectly attained, constantly approximated, and thereby constantly spreading and deepening its influence, and augmenting the happiness and value of life to all people of all colors everywhere. The assertion that 'all men are created equal' was of no practical use in effecting our separation from Great Britain; and it was placed in the Declaration, not for that, but for future use. Its authors meant it to be, thank God, it is now proving itself, a stumbling block to those who in after times might seek to turn a free people back into the hateful paths of despotism. They knew the proneness of prosperity to breed tyrants, and they meant when such should re-appear in this fair land and commence their vocation they should find left for them at least one hard nut to crack.[75]

But what about the Constitution? Why didn't the Constitution outlaw slavery? After all, it says at the very beginning that the Constitution was meant to "establish Justice" and "secure the Blessings of Liberty." Didn't Madison himself at the start of the Constitutional Convention say so tellingly that "we have seen the mere distinction of color made in the most enlightened period of time a ground of the most oppressive dominion ever exercised by man over man"?[76]

---

[75] Lincoln, "Speech on the Dred Scott Decision," June 26, 1857.

[76] Farrand, op. cit., p. 135.

Notice, again, the insistence by the Founders that slaves, despite their condition, were fully men, with all the natural rights of men everywhere. Today we often say, far too cavalierly, that we have to put people in "the context of their times." We often do this to excuse behavior that we think is wrong, while letting it be known that we surely wouldn't do such a thing today. So we say that because the Founders were people "of their time and place" they really didn't see the black man back then as a full human being. But this is clearly wrong. The humanity of the black race was completely understood by virtually everyone, especially by the Founders — and this is what made the Founders' choices so difficult, so complicated, and (in the area of slavery) so tragic for the future.

So how could the Founders, with all their fine words, not have abolished slavery when they had the chance?

First, as Lincoln notes, nothing Madison or Jefferson or the other major Founders wrote could have made South Carolina or Georgia abandon slavery. If the issue were pushed, those states and maybe others would not have joined in signing the Declaration and would not have joined the Union. Anything stronger might have seemed a great stand on principle, but it would not have freed one single slave.

Second, since the Founders could free no slave in any state without that state's consent, the best that could be done would be to bring all states into the union, in the hopes and expectation that slavery would one day, sooner rather than later, die out. Within two years of the Declaration of Independence, while we were still fighting the war with Great Britain, the Virginia General assembly banned the importation of all slaves.[77] Other slave states soon followed. Shortly

---

[77] Although it's unclear, Jefferson was probably the author of the bill.

thereafter, all the northern states began officially to abolish slavery within their boundaries.[78] And, just as the Constitution was being written in Philadelphia, the Continental Congress sitting under the Articles of Confederation passed the Northwest Ordinance, which forbade slavery in all the lands that would ultimately comprise the states of Ohio, Indiana, Illinois, Michigan, Wisconsin and parts of Minnesota. So it seemed possible, indeed probable to the Founders, that what they had begun by declaring the natural rights of all men to freedom would come true in the not too distant future.

With slavery so confined, the Founders could hold fast to the belief that slavery would be, in Lincoln's words, "in the course of ultimate extinction."[79]

So confident were the Founders in the ultimate extinction of slavery in America that the writers of the Constitution would not even allow the words "slave" or "slavery" to appear in the document. The idea of slavery was so dishonorable that, when generations in the future looked at the document, they should not be reminded that such an evil thing ever flourished in America.

---

[78] Vermont was the first officially to abolish slavery in 1777. Massachusetts and Pennsylvania followed in 1780. These were then followed by New Hampshire in 1783, Connecticut and Rhode Island in 1784, New York in 1799, and New Jersey in 1804.

[79] See Lincoln's "House Divided Speech," June 17, 1858. See, also, the Sixth Lincoln-Douglas Debate: "I insist that our fathers did not make this nation half slave and half free, or part slave and part free. I insist that they found the institution of slavery existing here. They did not make it so, but they left it so because they knew of no way to get rid of it at that time. When Judge Douglas undertakes to say that as a matter of choice the fathers of the government made this nation part slave and part free, he assumes what is historically a falsehood. More than that; when the fathers of the government cut off the source of slavery by the abolition of the slave trade, and adopted a system of restricting it from the new Territories where it had not existed, I maintain that they placed it where they understood, and all sensible men understood, it was in the course of ultimate extinction; and when Judge Douglas asks me why it cannot continue as our fathers made it, I ask him why he and his friends could not let it remain as our fathers made it?"

But what about the infamous "three-fifths" clause, which said that both representation and direct taxation was to be apportioned by fully counting all free persons but multiplying all others by three-fifths. Doesn't that make shambles out of "all men are created equal"? Well, no, not a bit. In fact, the truth is that, for purposes of representation in Congress, the free state delegates to the Philadelphia Convention didn't want slaves counted at all! It was the slave states that wanted their slaves counted as full people so that (even though slaves couldn't vote in the South) southern whites would have more representatives in Congress than the northern states did! Of course, when it came to being taxed, the tables turned. There it was the South that didn't want slaves counted as anything. So a compromise was reached on how to count slaves, a compromise that had nothing to do with their degree of personhood or humanity. It was merely a compromise number to force the slave states to pay some proportion of tax on their slaves while keeping them from using their slave population to boost even higher their numbers in Congress.

Still, it has to be said, that the calculation the Founders made — that slavery would soon wither away — was wrong. The Founders couldn't foresee the coming of the Louisiana Purchase, which would open new states to slavery, nor could they predict the invention of the cotton gin, which turned the ownership of personal and small-farm slaves into a vast plantation network. Sadly for the nation, it became clear that the problem of slavery could not be solved constitutionally but only extra-constitutionally, that is, by war.

Obviously, letting the Southern states "secede" from the Union might have avoided the War, but it would not in any way have solved the matter of slavery. It was only through a war fought at least in part to "make men free" (as the *Battle Hymn of the Republic* says) that led to the abolition of slavery. And the idea that all men deserve to be free exists in the American creed thanks to Jefferson's Declaration and Madison's Constitution.

Why did Lincoln and the Northern states consider secession illegitimate? As we all know, the war was fought as much if not more to maintain the Union as to free the slaves. Isn't secession a principle we can derive from the Declaration, and isn't the right of secession a reserved right of the states?

No and no. To be sure, if indeed there were states suffering under the actual tyranny of other states — their property confiscated, their citizens denied due process of law, their young men sent to fight while others left at home — then it is not only secession that would be called for but revolution itself. But no right was being denied the South by Lincoln's election. Indeed, the only rights that were being violated were being violated by and in the southern states themselves.

More broadly, the idea of secession strikes squarely against the very possibility of democratic government. If every time one side loses a vote they secede, then there cannot be democratic government at all. *While Madison and the Founders did all in their power to make democratic government as moderate and protective of rights as they could, in the end some form of the majority has to rule.*

To allow secession, especially in a nation with all the safeguards against tyranny that the Constitution built in, is to say that democracy is impossible anywhere — that a minority can walk off whenever it wishes. Or that a minority can *extort* concessions from a ruling majority by threatening to walk anytime they fear they might lose in a fair and constitutional vote. Then having made democracy impossible as a form of government, all that will be left is rule by kings or clergy or the powerful or thugs.

This is why Lincoln said in the Gettysburg Address that the real question is not whether a democracy could be established (of course it can, and was) but whether it could *endure*.

* * * * *

The issue of slavery highlights the fundamental tenuousness, even fragility, of the Founders' construct. In 1860 the nation was torn apart by the one thing Madison feared most — the division of the nation into two simply irreconcilable factions: free and slave. It was also blown apart by the belief that "secession" was a principle somehow compatible with constitutional democratic government, and undermined by a radicalized belief in a false "right" — the right of some men to own other men. And it was abetted in all this by a decision of the Supreme Court — *Dred Scott v. Sandford* — that said, falsely and tragically for the nation, that members of the black race were not men as understood by Jefferson's Declaration and that, under Madison's Constitution, they had no rights that a white man was obliged to respect.

The *Dred Scott* decision is important because it shows that Hamilton was correct in asserting that the whole Constitution in all its workings and complexity — and not the courts — was the best guarantor of our rights. The belief of many Americans that the courts are the real and ultimate defenders of rights is no more correct today than it was before the coming of the Civil War.

But all this naturally leads us to one final question: Exactly how are we to know what our rights are? Does someone tell us, or are we to work this question out for ourselves? Given the demand of our Founding that we both maintain our respect for democracy and democratic institutions as well as the protection of liberty and rights, the question remains: "How?"

I believe all Americans understand that liberty and rights are not static concepts. Hamilton was surely correct in thinking that trying to catalogue all our rights would be a fool's errand. Moreover, who can predict how rights will grow to cover new situations, like the coming of radio or television — or how we might need to regulate them in an age of internet piracy, the rise of international terrorism, or weapons of mass destruction?

To say, "Well, the courts, especially the Supreme Court, will decide what rights we have and what their limits are," is, as I hope has been shown, a serious mistake. Nothing in the Founders' Constitution points to the courts in general or the Supreme Court in particular as the sole or even primary expounder of our rights.[80] While the Supreme Court plays an important role in helping us govern ourselves, it is exactly that: it "helps" us govern. It does not, in the most important things, govern us.

Historically, the Court has been as often wrong about our rights as it has been supportive. When the nation, in response to *Dred Scott* and secession passed the Thirteenth, Fourteenth, and Fifteenth Amendments permanently freeing all slaves, clothing the freedman with all the privileges of American citizenship, and expressly protecting his right to vote, the Court not only turned these amendments around so as to make them meaningless for the freedman but it also used its power to overturn all the early Civil

---

[80] See John Agresto, *The Supreme Court and Constitutional Democracy* (Ithaca: Cornell University Press, 1984).

Rights acts that Congress passed to secure the rights of the black race.[81]

But it is not just a bad history that disqualifies the Court from being the final or infallible word on our rights. The whole theory of constitutional democracy works to hold the Court at bay.

It cannot be said often enough that the Founders used every device they could to see to it that all national legislative majorities were as broadly based, moderate, and non-despotic as human inventiveness could politically invent. The Founders went so far as to push hard in the opposite direction: The national government leans more often towards inaction and slowness, even gridlock, than towards excessive haste and ill-considered actions. Because of the various limitations on power built into our government, because of our pluralistic nature, and because of the redundancy built into the system, slowness is more often the hallmark of our system than speed.

Part of this redundancy, this system of checks and balances, is the Supreme Court. It is one of the institutions that can and does force us to take a sober second look at our legislation. Still, while it is part of the system of checks and balances, it is not the whole of the system. When the courts — including the Supreme

---

[81] Consider *U.S. v Cruikshank*, which declared that the rights of life, liberty, assembly, and the franchise were not federal rights at all and so could not be protected by Congress. Or *U.S. v. Harris*, which threw out the Federal 1871 Anti-Lynching Act. Or *The Civil Rights Cases*, decided in 1883, which forbade Congress from outlawing discrimination in public accommodations, conveyances, and places of public amusement. The Court even went so far, in *U.S .v. Reese,* to invalidate a federal statute that had forbidden state election officials from denying to any person entitled to do so the right to cast a vote, thus not only making a travesty of the Fifteenth Amendment but also of the words carefully appended to the end of all three post-Civil War Amendments, namely, "The Congress shall have power to enforce this article by appropriate legislation." Thus the three post-Civil War Amendments, passed in large part to undo the damage a renegade Court did in *Dred Scott,* were turned against the Congress that wrote and passed them and into vehicles for increased, some might say unlimited, Court power.

Court — make mistakes, it is the constitutional duty of the people and their representatives to press the issue.

Some of this pushback we all know, and it goes well beyond amending the Constitution to overturn a Court decision. For example, the president both can and should nominate people to the federal bench who will interpret the Constitution as he or she understands it. The Senate has an equal obligation to see to it that nominated members of the court understand the Senate's view of the Constitution and the needs of the nation. The Senate is under no obligation to give its consent blindly.

Moreover, as we learned in the struggle to expand civil rights in the '60s, Congress has its own authority to promote legislation, despite long-standing, historic Supreme Court cases to the contrary. Or the states, reflecting the views of their citizens, can respond to unpopular or erroneous Supreme Court decisions until an appropriate understanding is reached. This is exactly what the states and to a degree the federal government have been doing to moderate and ultimately change *Roe v. Wade*. Every new piece of legislation — on waiting times, on clinic requirements, on procedures to be followed, and so on — all legitimately and constitutionally test and push the limits of that unfortunate decision.

Throughout all this give and take between the more popular and democratic elements of our republic and the courts, the constitutional principle is clear: The Supreme Judiciary is there to review our laws and help us live up to the ideals we set out for ourselves in the Constitution; it is not there to make our laws.

While it is to help us make our rule better, the Supreme Court is not there to rule in its own name. It may have the last word in any particular case and be the governor of inferior court, but it is not our supreme ruler, nor are the other branches merely inferior branches. Lincoln's words in his First Inaugural are most perhaps the most apt:

> If the policy of the government upon vital questions affecting the whole people is to be irrevocably fixed by decisions of the Supreme Court the instant they are made ... the people will have ceased to be their own rulers, having to that extent practically resigned their government into the hands of that eminent tribunal.

We must always remember it was a restrained, representative, constitutional democracy that the Founders gave us, not governance under the least democratic branch in the nation. Nor should we be beguiled by the notion that the Court is there to save us from "the tyranny of the majority." While it is surely true that the Founders worried about the dangers of majority tyranny, they were even more alarmed by the idea of "*minority* tyranny" — within which we certainly can put rule by judges.

* * * * *

All this is a long and complex way of bringing us back to the main focus of this chapter on rights: That the last word regarding our rights lies with the totality of the political process set out in our Constitution, not in any presumed privileged part of it.[82]

---

[82] To refer again to Madison: "In the extended republic of the United States, and among the great variety of interests, parties, and sects which it embraces, a coalition of a majority could seldom take place on any other principles than those of justice and the general good...." To which, Madison immediately adds, apropos of the Court or any other supposed non-democratic check, "whilst there being thus less danger to a minor from the will of a major party, there must be less pretext, also, to provide for the security of the former by introducing into the government a will not dependent on the latter, or, in other words, a will independent of the society itself." *Federalist,* No. 51.

So how do we recognize new rights or the expansion of already existing rights, and, most especially, how do we understand what might be the appropriate extent or limits to our rights? The answer is *through the fullness of the democratic process the Founders bequeathed to us.* WE — not the Court, not the President, not the *Harvard Law Review* — decide the shape and direction of our political lives through our votes, our deliberations, and the checks and balances of all our institutions working constitutionally.

Consider, for example, what a democratic and constitutional approach might be to a serious and contemporary issue: the issue of same-sex marriages. Although philosophers might debate whether anyone can claim a natural right to engage in acts widely and historically understood as "contrary to nature," no one can legitimately say that homosexuals as people have fewer basic rights than all others. No matter what one's sexual orientation, the rights to life, liberty, property, the pursuit of happiness, safety, security, and so on belong to *all* persons, not just straight persons. This means, for example, that all the laws newly passed in Uganda, Kenya, Russia, and elsewhere that make it a crime to be homosexual or associate with them or demand that others report them to the authorities are utterly unjust.

That women can live with women or men with men, that they are free to share their lives and their fortunes, that they may care for one another and love one another, is not a matter of public concern. In this, as in what occupation people choose or to what faith they adhere, all people are free, equal, and independent.

But when two (or, arguably, more) wish for their bond to be publicly denominated and sanctioned as "marriage" by a community, then that community, that public, might well have a part to play. In this, the people at large might legitimately say that, yes, they approve of these arrangements and wish to give each party the legal protections and liabilities that all married couples have. But it is equally true that the public may say that it has real, historic, and socially appropriate reasons to reserve "marriage" for the union of men and women; or that it wishes to underscore the value of joining the qualities of male and female in its understanding of families; or that it wishes to honor that arrangement upon which the regeneration of all society depends; or simply that it is not comfortable in overturning the accumulated wisdom of virtually all nations, all cultures, and all religions so quickly and without long and serious thought.

In the end, whatever the reasons, whether solid or spurious, when it comes to expanding our understanding of rights, the argument of this chapter is that it is not the opinion of courts or the wishes of judges and lawyers alone that matter. Before the people can be told that they must call this or that arrangement "marriage" and clothe it with all the honor and benefits that go with that term, it must be in largest part *their* decision.

Yes, this issue will rile up the nation and unleash a hard and wide-ranging debate. Good. It will force people to think about what their beliefs are and why. Good. It will mean that whatever decision they come to will not only be theirs but it can also be reconsidered by them if the argument turns the other way. Good. And none of these goods will occur if Americans are told that they cannot deliberate and decide for themselves the meaning, extent, and coverage of their rights but that it will be decided for them by appointed judges. Any other avenue of decision is an affront both to the people's right to deliberate about their rights individually and collectively, and an affront to the constitutional system the Founders took such pains to construct.

* * * * *

We are a nation dedicated to the ever-expanding, ever-deepening understanding of what a life lived under the commands of the laws of Nature and Nature's God might be. We are a people looking to mesh the rights of each of us with the rights of all of us. We are a country that not only hopes to secure the blessings of liberty but to do so without sacrificing all the other goods the Constitution hopes to help us achieve: peace, prosperity, the common good, national security, and justice. But how do we work towards these ends? In only one way: not by handing over our futures and our liberty to any court, not by trust in the beneficence of any executive — but by governing ourselves through a complex democratic framework of representation, oversight, checks, and balances, all within a nation that is large, pluralistic, and diverse, with a people the Founders hoped would be moderated in its outlook and restrained in its pursuits. It is this extraordinary mix of a restrained democracy with a moderated and decent citizenry working through overlapping and checking institutions that has made the American promise of liberty and justice for all unprecedented in all history.

Will we, as a constitutional democracy, make mistakes? No doubt, at times. But they will be our mistakes, not mistakes imposed on us extra-democratically. Will we remedy our mistakes? If history is any guide, probably more easily and quickly than court-ordered or bureaucratically decreed mistakes.

In the end, this is why Hamilton was surely correct: In every rational sense and for every useful purpose it has been the Founders' Constitution that has been not only the protector of our liberties but the engine of our prosperity, of our security, and the promoter of justice as well.

- VI -

Liberty, Equality, and the Character of American Life

I BEGAN THIS BOOK describing how I saw Iraqis, who had just been liberated from a most brutal dictatorship, turn slowly from a love affair with American freedom to an almost tangible retreat from what they first thought they wanted. Their reasons were fairly clear: They were discovering that things they had relied on throughout the centuries to secure, support, and give meaning to their lives — namely religion, tradition, and family — were the very things that our version of democracy seemed to them bent on eroding.

When I first thought seriously about this,[83] my immediate reaction was that of any good American: "They just aren't seeing it right." I understood that the principle of equal liberty had cultural implications, but its ramifications seemed, in the abstract, almost always beneficial. For example, the coming of liberal democracy would subvert a culture of tyranny and political oppression and impart to the human spirit a robust independence and a greater sense of worth. Moreover, I knew that the blessings of equal liberty included the grand promise that everyone, men and women alike, could become whatever their talents, ambition, and effort might finally have in store for them, and thus increase both individual and societal well-being. I also knew that freedom meant freedom

---

[83] John Agresto, *Mugged by Reality: The Liberation of Iraq and the Failure of Good Intentions* (New York: Encounter Books, 2007).

from religious domination and oppression, turning men's understanding of religion from fear to attachment. But it was now painfully apparent that my appreciation of the consequences of liberty and equality — or, at least, our inadequate contemporary notions of liberty and equality — had been too sanguine, too optimistic.

My original reaction to the abuses at Abu Ghraib was similar. When I first wrote about the event, I tried to explain that what we did there was surely an aberration. During my time overseas, I found much to blame in Iraqi culture. But when it came to the odious and indefensible conduct of some Americans, I tried to excuse it as the random acts of renegade individuals, not as something with modern political and cultural roots. But some reviewers took me to task for this, and they were right to do so. There is, it must be said, something amiss — seriously amiss — in contemporary American life.

Of course we needn't go abroad to sense the problem. I hope I understand and appreciate the decency and actual goodness of so many of our fellow citizens. But our virtues, real as they are, are not the whole story. Are we still an independent and self-reliant people? Do we still have a good understanding of the responsibilities that come with the enjoyment of our rights? When we look at American culture and mores, what shall we make of the coarseness and the hypersexualization of so much of today's culture? Were my Middle Eastern friends right in thinking that neither childhood nor family life could withstand the giddy joys of such an onslaught? Or is freedom just another word for the liberation of our baser natures, the release of those desires that civilization and religion took centuries to try to tame? How shall we understand the effects, both positive and negative, of liberal democracy on our souls?

* * * * *

The Founders knew that human nature could be turned or improved only so much. I'm not sure they would have fully agreed with George Will that "statecraft" was "soulcraft" — that political forms could deeply change our natures. But they did think elements of our character could be improved. They did think that liberty and equality — coupled with the political institutions they established and the various civic and religious institutions that flourished under freedom — would enable us to live together more or less peacefully and with increased justice.

But first look at the almost impossible task they set out for themselves: They took ordinary men and women, with all the defects, iniquities, and limitations of their common human natures, and set them free to be whatever they would be. The institutions they created protected the rights of all to produce, possess, and enjoy, but without governmental censors or overseers mandating charity or demanding neighborliness. Our Founders gave to these selfsame people — us — rule over an entire nation, responsibility for the future of our fellow citizens. And they thought the nation they created would still be peaceful, just, unified, and conducive to the general welfare.

Think of all the evil we should expect from such an arrangement. If men are, as Hamilton once decried, "ambitious, vindictive, and rapacious,"[84] would we not get a nation of vicious souls — of "rapacious," grasping, and selfish predators — rather than of potential friends and fellow citizens? Combine this with our de-

---

[84] *Federalist*, No. 6.

votion to commerce and prosperity, our love of private property, our belief in the centrality of rights, and our devotion to limited, that is, non-interfering government — why should we not expect America to be a nation of crude, materialistic and self-interested brutes whose country would be as ugly as it was short-lived?

Add to that the many different races, ethnicities, and competing religions in America with all the tensions and frictions their living together might engender. Yes, Madison taught us to expand the boundaries of the nation and purposely take in the greatest variety of human types, interests, and faiths, with the expectation that, being politically unable to oppress one another, they might learn how to tolerate and accommodate each other. But it was all untried, all an experiment. It was to be, as Madison noted, "a system without precedent, ancient or modern."[85]

Without sugarcoating the historical record, I would offer that the experiment has so far been a success, and a success on many levels. Our Founders managed to establish a government that proved that rule by the people need not be chaotic, ignorant, or unjust. They proved that men and women could be could be free without being simply "rapacious" towards one another. They proved that a free people could still be a patriotic people — men and women devoted to their neighbors, their fellow citizens, and to an ideal.

Perfect? Hardly. But if you want to see how exceptional America is in this regard, just look on every other continent.[86]

---

[85] *The Records of the Federal Convention*, op. cit., Volume 3, p. 539 (Madison's "Preface to the Debates in the Federal Convention of 1787").

[86] Consider, similarly, Thomas Paine: "If there is a country in the world where concord, according to common calculation, would be least expected, it is America. Made up as it is of people from different nations, accustomed to different forms and habits of government, speaking different languages, and more different in their modes of worship, it would appear that the union of such a people was impracticable; but by the simple operation of constructing government on the prin-

Still the question arises, "How?" How is it that the statecraft of the Founders had the effect of both freeing and restraining us at the same time? How is it possible that we have managed, at least historically, to turn a love of individual liberty into a great social good?

To unravel this paradox, we need to begin again with the self-evident truths of the Declaration: The idea that all men are created equal, supported by almost two centuries of religious teachings, pushes us to look beyond the universal human tendency to love one's own and despise the "other," and instead to begin seeing others as similar to ourselves. As Lincoln noted, the belief that all men are created equal was hardly something that had to be said for us to declare our independence from Great Britain. No, it was written because it was both a truth evident to every self as well as an idea upon which we should and would understand ourselves as a people. This truth of human equality was, as Lincoln also so powerfully said, "the father of all moral principle" in us.[87] We are not a nation based on one stock or one religious heritage, but on one idea, that of the equality of right. It is that idea — that none of us is by God or nature superior to any other — that is the moral ground of our ties of sympathy, respect, and often affection for our neighbor. And when this idea of human equality was denied, as it was during the Civil War, how many thousands upon thousands of Americans selflessly gave their lives to re-vivify that truth?

---

ciples of society and the rights of man, every difficulty retires, and all the parts are brought into cordial unison." The premise is true, and the consequences still remarkable, even if we set aside such hyperboles as "every difficulty retires." *The Rights of Man*, Ch. I, paragraph 14.

[87] Lincoln, "Speech at Chicago, Illinois," July 10, 1858. Reprinted in the Appendix to this book, p. 224.

I still clearly remember a conversation I had with an Iraqi academic who repeated the line that all we Americans wanted from Iraq was their oil. I tried to tell him that if we had wanted their oil, we could have bought it from Saddam for a small fraction of what the war was costing us in treasure and blood. In fact, I added, most of the Americans I knew who were working in Iraq were actually looking to help. At that he laughed. "Help," he said — no one goes abroad "to help." Such a thing was unnatural. People don't willingly help others, especially not strangers. And, if it were true that America wanted to help people who were not connected to them, then Americans were "stupid." After all, he said with real candor, *We would never do that for you.*" In that he was right; neither they nor any others would do it for us. We Americans truly are different.

How often the world imagines that we Americans are just like them — and how little like them we actually are. The rest of the world cannot imagine that our foreign policy might actually have more than our own interests and security involved — that we might also have the interests and freedom of other people at heart. The rebuilding of Germany and Japan? The Marshall Plan? The support we gave for the liberation of Eastern Europe? The war we helped wage in Kosovo to free Muslims from repression and genocide? The fight against Saddam in both Kuwait and Iraq? Were these all simply because of oil or calculated self-interest? Or is there not some *idea* embedded in the American mind that understands the natural right of everyone to live freely as a moral command?

Have we always behaved with charity and grace? No, of course not. But all I know is that, in Iraq, whenever a bomb went off, every Iraqi in the area ran away from the blast to save himself. It was only human. Yet every American GI in the area would run towards the blast, hoping to save his comrades. It was only American.

* * * * *

What this foundational idea of equal liberty has accomplished in America is largely counterintuitive. How is it possible that we have liberated men and freed them to pursue their own interests, and wound up with a nation where so many are so committed to the protection of the rights of all? How can we proclaim the inalienable rights of life, liberty, and the pursuit of happiness yet find so many Americans truly and sincerely patriotic — that is, willing to give up their lives and liberty so that their country will survive and their fellow citizens live and prosper? Moreover, why do we always swagger and say that all we are really interested in is "Number One" — and then wind up building hospitals, supporting international orphanages, battling AIDS and Ebola in Africa, and even dying as we topple tyrants and despots halfway across the globe? How is it that a philosophy that proclaims the primacy of each individual can ever result in generosity, self-denying friendship, and those many acts of compassion each of us sees every day?

It would be good to remind ourselves of that day not so long ago when the planes flew into the Twin Towers. Beyond the picture of the falling buildings, perhaps the image most seared into our American memories is of policemen and firemen running UP the stairs of the towers while everyone else was running down. They ran up, and they died. Why did they run into those burning and crashing buildings? To save their neighbors, neighbors they didn't know, neighbors many of them would never meet.

Some of this love of neighbor is traceable to more than 2,000 years of religious teachings. But our concern for our neighbor goes beyond reliance on our religious heritage. Most of our fellow citizens who profess no religion themselves are fully respectful, tolerant, and charitable to their neighbors. And this is surely because of what we know not just from our religious creeds but from our *American* creed.

Beyond our understanding of the truth of human equality, even our very attachment to liberty and property has had a salutary moral effect. If our sense of equality encourages us to treat our neighbor as we would treat ourselves, in an odd way our belief in freedom leads us down much the same path. We saw some of how this worked in the earlier chapter on economics and justice. Of course, the common good is reached not by people first looking to help their neighbors but simply looking to help themselves. This is what Adam Smith meant by the "invisible hand." In seeking the satisfaction of their own desires, the butcher, the baker, and the brewer are led — as if by an invisible hand — to help other people satisfy their needs as well. But achieving the wider good in material terms is only part of the story. Free exchange often has a *moral* effect on the seller, on the buyer, and on all society.

For example, a butcher who puts his thumb on the scale may very well get caught. And if he's caught and his customers go elsewhere, his business will be ruined. So calculation and self-interest push individuals towards honesty. In this way honesty seems right not because it's good or virtuous but because it's the best "policy." But what began in calculation soon becomes a habit, and after a while people find themselves less tempted to cheat. In fact, they like having a reputation for honesty, and want to keep it. So what began in self-interest soon becomes morality. Similarly, neighbors often help their neighbors build a garage or fence not because they particularly like them but because of a calculation that the favor might be returned tomorrow. But helping others becomes a habit. And, little by little, the rust of selfishness wears off.

But our beliefs have more than an effect how we view others. *They have had a pivotal effect on how we understand ourselves.* Yes, when we see others suffering an unwarranted hardship, we easily can put ourselves in their place, and very often do. But it goes even further than that: Because we know, deep down, that all men are created equal, we Americans do not begin with the expectation that others are there to serve us. We do not begin with the idea of privilege — that we "deserve" to be supported or that others have an obligation to help us.

Thanks to our national emphasis on equality and freedom, on self-reliance and individual effort, we almost instinctively react against being treated as dependent beings. We prize our independence. Historically, the majority of Americans have had no interest in being wards of the government. It may seem paradoxical, but free people both lift themselves up *and* support their neighbors.

I was in Missouri in 2011, just after a multiple vortex EF-5 tornado hit the town of Joplin. It was the deadliest recorded tornado in American history, with over 1,300 casualties and thousands of homes and businesses wiped away. Still, perhaps the most amazing thing about Joplin — and it's a story repeated thousands of times before and since in the American heartland — is that, when disaster struck, neighbor ran to help neighbor. Before government relief agencies could arrive, people's devotion to their fellow citizens overwhelmed their instinct to look out only for themselves. Strangers took in wandering children. Neighbors dug out neighbors still alive in the rubble. People who still had kitchens cooked food and fed and helped the newly homeless. With the hospital destroyed, nurses walked about, caring for the injured in the streets. Again, a free people, raised with the philosophical belief in the equality of all men and aided by tradition and faith, seem ready not only to lift themselves up but support their neighbors as well.

There are, of course, places in America where the story reads somewhat differently. Places where looting, not mutual help, is more often than not the aftermath of tragedy. Places where self-reliance seems less powerful a factor than waiting for government support and assistance. What might be partially behind these two widely differing responses we shall presently try to discover.

* * * * *

Why talk at such length about our American character — both our regard for others and our historical self-reliance — in a book on the politics and philosophy of the Founding? Well, insofar as our principles have been productive of a certain culture and a certain type of individual distinctly "American," a radical change in the meaning and understanding of those principles will produce a people of a different sort. That is, as we modify our understanding of our great principles we will change our character as Americans. And the change will hardly be for the better.

Recall how Justice Ginsburg told the Egyptians that she preferred the South African constitution to her own when it came to protecting rights. Why South Africa? Because, the estimable Justice opined, the South African constitution truly "embraces basic human rights." Their constitution demands that the government *supply* as "rights" free universal education, housing, access to health care (including free reproductive health care), welfare for the needy, and even protection from others speaking poorly about us. By contrast, our Constitution is so limited, so negative in its concept of rights. It protects our right to lead our own lives and take responsibility for our own happiness but avoids using government to give us all the supposedly fine things of life.

No doubt Justice Ginsburg believes her thoughts are more advanced and just than the Founders'. They are certainly more contemporary. But does she fully understand why the Founders, who could have placed these and other more "positive" rights in the Constitution, did not? Does she understand why a transformation of Americans from an independent to a dependent people is likely to be one of the most destructive things for our nation and for our character? Does she understand why we have survived as a free people for over two centuries, while those nations that look to government to make them happy so quickly have become international tragedies? Apparently not.

* * * * *

What might be the consequences of ever-increased dependence on government? What might result from this new understanding of equality as perpetual support, where rising is suspect but falling is prevented, or where liberty is prized so long as it doesn't discomfort anyone else? Or, to concentrate directly on character, how does a more active, paternal and overseeing government make us a different people?

The consequences of such a change in our political lives has been known for almost two centuries. To return again to Tocqueville, such an active and paternal government stands over its people as "an immense and tutelary power," a power always there

> to secure their gratifications and to watch over their fate. That power is absolute, minute, regular, provident, and mild. It would be like the authority of a parent if, like that authority, its object was to prepare men for manhood; but it seeks, on the contrary, to keep them in perpetual childhood. ... For their happiness such a government willingly labors. ... [I]t provides for their security, foresees and supplies their necessities, facilitates their pleasures, manages their principal concerns, directs their industry, regulates the descent of property, and subdivides their inheritances: What remains, but to spare them all the care of thinking and all the trouble of living?[88]

American liberals and progressives will always tend to view governmental activity and governmental regulations more favorably than American conservatives do. And conservatives will, generally, look more favorably on strengthening private, civic, and religious groups and giving wider berth for their activities. Often government action *is* more "efficient." Nor is such paternalism always heavy-handed. As Tocqueville noted, it often looks to all the world as both "provident and mild."

Is governmental action sometimes an absolute imperative? Yes, of course. But when government substitutes for our own efforts, clothing us with "rights" to ordinary health care, welfare payments, housing, perpetual food stamps, free contraception, or protection from the disrespect of others, government action does

---

[88] Alexis de Tocqueville, *Democracy in America*, Volume II, book 4, chapter IV.

little to help form "free, equal, and independent" citizens.

Government acting on our behalf, supplying our various needs and helping satisfy our many desires, will do little to better our character or shape our souls for good. How could it? Government doing for us what we, together, can and should do for ourselves disconnects us from community and depresses personal responsibility. Even worse, government action in place of private acts far too often teaches a debilitating and an ultimately destructive sense of dependency. It turns us, as Tocqueville also said, from citizens back to subjects.

Relying on public support for the satisfaction of our needs goes far deeper than the problem of government subsidies for the poor and disadvantaged. For instance, it is often the children of the rich and the upper-middle-class, those who have been born thinking that somehow they are "owed," who are the worst examples of this spirit of entitlement. Often it was the children and grandchildren of those who fought in World War II — sons and daughters raised with their wants and needs supplied, who grew up expecting that the best education would be given to them, their loans covered, all physical enjoyments available, their health and ease assured, their "self-esteem" cultivated, their "values" praised, and their character fawned over — who turned their back on the ordinary morals and work ethic of the nation. From the SDS, the counter-culture, the flower children, and the anti-war zealots all the way through the "occupy" crowd — all those with their hands out and their middle fingers raised — it is these who not only look for others to satisfy their demands but who also flatter themselves as the embodiment of some finer morality.

How often are we told that those who agitate, demonstrate, and organize for greater redistribution or more collectivism are finer, more caring people than those who work in the day, pay their bills, feed their kids, and watch TV in the evening. Protestors, we're told, are people who truly care for the downtrodden and love humanity, people who will save our planet, people who live on a higher moral plane than the rest of us. Unlike most of us, who only learn to be virtuous by working hard at it day by day, those who push for equalizing the wealth or whatever form of communal policies seem right this year, seem to be virtuous by nature, virtuous in their hearts.

But what have we witnessed at the various street rallies, university shutdowns, occupations, and demonstrations? Claims of entitlement. Chants of envy, resentment, anger, and hate. Smashed windows, overturned cars, and destroyed businesses. Statements that, unless society gives in to their idea of "justice," there will be no peace. And soon we begin to understand that those who believe that they are "owed" by others, that they are "entitled" to their fair share without their having to do or produce, are often far worse in morals and character than ordinary bourgeois working stiffs.

What happens in those supposedly more virtuous places where welfare is owed and the expectation that others are morally bound to take care of you has become the rule? Exactly what we see in socialist Europe as it declines, or the street gangs of Britain, or the worst elements of the organized entitlement crowd here in our country: When things do not go well, it's always the fault of others — the wealthy, the powerful, the Jews, those selfish and racist Americans. All of these "others" have too much money, aren't sharing, are unjust, are keeping you down. And, since it's their fault that you are poorer than they, and their fault you are not "fairly" being taken care of, we have not only the politics of resentment and envy but the politics of anger and of hatred. And it's hard to make anger and hate into virtues, no matter how much their adherents vaunt the superiority of their morals.

We should never forget that the nations that look not only to promote "liberté" and "égalité" but to enforce "fraternité" — so warming and pleasant-sounding — wind up with the guillotine and the Terror. Nor should we forget that, throughout the 20th century, those countries that called themselves "socialist" of one stripe or another are responsible for the deaths of more than 100 million people.

In the end, the various ideologies that struggle to "equalize" humans and redistribute their possessions find that they can only do it through force, often the most oppressive totalitarian force. Sadly, captured by their ideology, the worst of these states think that such a project is totally acceptable, perfectly just.

Here is the crux of the deep moral problem with modern radical egalitarianism: Those who wish to have what others have worked for, those who think there should be "preferential options" for their kind and those they favor, those who believe that they are "entitled" to have their desires satisfied *can only see others as means and not as ends*. They can only see that others have what they do not, others possess what they want, and they command its redistribution to them. And that principle — *that others are means and not ends, that others must give when we demand* — is the father not of generosity of spirit, not of love of neighbor, but, rather, of the worst immorality.

This moral disaster ties directly into the radical egalitarian notion that "fairness" involves rewarding people more "equally" and not, as the Founders understood, on the basis of their merit or their work or their productiveness and inventiveness. This is the destructive trajectory of our revised and radicalized notion of what "equality" means.

* * * * *

But a misunderstanding of liberty is working to change our national character just as surely as a misunderstanding of equality has. It has been this modern misunderstanding of the meaning of rights that has helped make the noble idea of liberty increasingly unattractive to so much of the rest of the world. And it has been, moreover, a misunderstanding, a radicalization, that has been supported by elements on both the "libertarian" right and the "civil liberties" left.

The last 50 years have seen a virtual explosion of "rights." Some of these rights are important outgrowths of the core idea of human liberty championed by the Founders, rights that only recently have been able to flower fully. In this area one must surely count the rights of all races to equal (not preferential) treatment, the right not to be segregated in school or barred from the voting booth, and the right of women to serve on juries and have all the same legal protections as men.

But we also know that, under the umbrella of "new" rights such as privacy, expression, and sexual freedom, much has changed. An expansive view of new privacy rights has led directly to the legalization of abortion and to all the challenges and roadblocks placed in the way of limiting the practice. New views on freedom of speech have made information gathering in the interests of national defense ever more difficult. These new views on freedom of speech coupled with "privacy" and "expression" rights have made restrictions on everything from access to obscene material to weapon and bomb-making information increasingly difficult to monitor and restrict.

All of this has not only public policy but cultural implications as well. All these new "rights" challenge and change the very character of the culture. As everyone knows, the cultivation of these rights in the current digital age has meant a major upsurge in pornography, in violent and sadistic music and videos, in rap lyrics glorifying rape and cop-killing — and full and easy access to these materials not simply to adults but to children and adolescents as well.

Nor is it simply or even primarily the left that champions these new liberties — greater liberality in the tolerance of drug use (and not just marijuana), for instance, and a more absolutist view of both "gun rights" and of the right to protect oneself from all types of governmental "intrusions" are hallmarks of a new and powerful libertarian movement on the right.

Perhaps the strangest aspect of the growth of these putative new rights is the way they undermine and often displace the enjoyment of other rights — rights rooted in our history and long protected, we thought, by the Constitution. Do parents have the right to bury their children without being picketed by lunatics carrying signs saying "Thank God for Dead Soldiers"? No, apparently not. Can parents have their public libraries limit access to weapon sites or put pornography filters on their open computers used by their children after school? No. Can Catholic adoption agencies limit their foster care and adoption placements to traditionally married couples? Not in Massachusetts, Illinois, or in the nation's capital. Can students be prevented from offering prayers at public events? Yes. Can students be suspended for vulgar language, inappropriate dress, or wearing tee-shirts that say "Fuck the Draft"? Probably not.

All these new rights have left large swaths of the culture in tatters. Because of our historic devotion to the idea of rights, ordinary citizens find themselves browbeaten if they try to object, as they often do, to the radical liberalization of the culture. What could be more "un-American" (they are told) than to be against freedom of speech — all speech — or against freedom of expression, any expression? And so the coarsening of the culture moves on at an ever-increasing pace.

One of the worst results of the modern expansion and radicalization of rights — and the one perhaps most noticed by more traditional societies abroad — has been the effect on religion. While a regard for our responsibilities and obligations always instructs us to think about others, rights in themselves are generally more internally directed — they speak to *our* life, *our* freedom, *our* property and possessions, *our* happiness, the achievement of *our* goals. Yes, as we have seen, a kind of morality does result from rights and self-interest rightly understood. But it is also the case that a just society has always needed more than simply an attachment to individual rights to prosper. If all I do is stand on my rights, why would I — as so many Americans so often do — sacrifice for my neighbors? Why would I give of my possessions to improve their lives or risk my own life to protect theirs? Why would I voluntarily vote for taxes that help others more than me? What keeps so many of us from cheating when we can, lying when its in our interest, and taking when we can get away with it? Oftentimes it's religion.

Yes, our belief in the equality of all men has been fundamental in bettering our moral lives. But I also do not doubt that religious teachings and the belief in a God who rewards the just and charitable and punishes the wicked have been pivotal in restraining the more self-interested and unpleasant aspects of our common natures. Which means that it is worrisome in the extreme that our current attacks on religion as everything from narrow-minded and bigoted to corrosive of freedom and contrary to science simply remove from the culture one of the historically most effective ways of restraining our mere self-interest.

The constant call of most organized religions in the West to virtue and to improve the content of our character is the great historical counterweight to the more self-regarding concerns of our contemporary lives. On their own, liberty, rights, and even prosperity may seem useful for happiness, but none are sufficient. We are happy in the bosom of our families, with the comfort of friends, and in the knowledge that we are trying to live the best life we can. Like families, religion teaches us to go beyond ourselves, to care for others, and love them as we love ourselves. Good old-fashioned organized religion has done much to make freedom more than mere self-interest. It has done much to help make liberty lovely.

But consider how religion and traditional morality are now widely seen as the enemies of freedom. Despite hospitals, soup kitchens, shelters for the abused, orphanages, schools, adoption agencies, refugee services, help for the grieving, and hope for the bereaved, our Western religious heritage has become, in too many parts of the culture, synonymous not with charity but illiberal rigidity and even hate. Soon, the strongest thing in helping us preserve the fundamentals of an obligation- and responsibility-respecting society against the onslaughts of our rights-dominated culture will be swept aside. And the view abroad in the world — that America has made liberty and "rights" the enemy of religion and moral character — will be reinforced, and all to the detriment not only of this country but of liberty itself.

This disparagement of religion, so popular in sophisticated America, is often put in terms of "extremism." Ordinary religious adherents find themselves painted as anti-women zealots or anti-modern fanatics — intolerant extremists who would impose their puritanical moral views on the more carefree denizens of modern life. Of course, condemning those who simply stand by older ideas of decent behavior and self-restraint as "religious extremists" is rather peculiar. Extremism in religion is beheading people who dare to question or who wish to convert. Intolerance is killing schoolchildren because someone somewhere drew a picture of Muhammad. Fanaticism is looking to wipe Israel off the face of the earth. Yet how many American Presbyterians or Mormons or Catholics or those derided as "fundamentalists" by their own countrymen commit any of those acts? Sadly, it often seems that the most extreme and intolerant among us are those who would falsely try to brand ordinary fellow citizens with those words.

* * * * *

Nevertheless, even though our "extremism" pales before the fanaticism we see growing in all corners of the world today, we cannot overlook how polarized, how uncompromising, even how hate-filled certain aspects of our public life seems to have become. Are most Americans these days "extremists"? Of course not. If anything, the characteristic of most Americans is their middling nature and their distrust of all extremes. But it would be foolish to ignore the fact that large and important swaths of America today view politics and social life as a battleground, and who see moderation and compromise as part of the problem.

We should remind ourselves that the most historically powerful argument against democracy was that popular governments were, by nature, turbulent, immoderate, and fanatical. In the face of that, Madison promised that one of the hallmarks of the new Constitution would be its moderation. But if the Constitution and the institutional arrangements it established wind up being no defense against "interested and overbearing" factionalism, if the character and communal spirit of American life is in the process of become seriously attenuated, then we have lost one of the most important promises of our Founders' Constitution.

Fifty years ago, Sen. Barry Goldwater kicked off his presidential campaign by declaring that moderation in the pursuit of liberty was no vice and extremism in the pursuit of justice no virtue. The thought that a presidential candidate would praise zealotry in any form—even for the sake of liberty and virtue — struck most Americans as bizarre, and Goldwater's candidacy was soon soundly rejected. Yet within a few short years extremism, not in speech but this time in action, grew to be part of the landscape of politics. The rise of the New Left, the Black Panthers, eco-terrorism, fires in ghettoes, the firebombing of black churches, urban terrorist attacks over the Vietnam War, political assassinations, the takeover of university campuses ... the fanaticism of the '60s and '70s retreated over the next few years, only to be resurrected by the wars in Afghanistan and especially Iraq and the economic dislocations of the new century.

As with the coming of the Civil War a mere four score and seven years after our Founding, these new divisions, these latest accretions of extremism, have both large and small causes. When the major parties were captured by those who thought that being ideologically pure and unbending was more important than broad-based accommodation, both electoral politics and reasonable public policy suffered. When the courts, following the lead of the Supreme Court, declared that Madison's idea of large, diverse electoral districts was unfair to minority candidates, identity politics grew, and cross-factional, cross-racial accommodation became less and less the norm. When, rather than evaluating a candidate's ideas and policy positions, even decent U.S. senators turned the confirmation processes into something akin to a third-world blood sport, the whole republic was harmed.

And so it has come to pass exactly as we could have expected: When smears and contempt become the norm, intelligent men and women of goodwill turn aside from politics and public service. Then only the most radical or ungoverned on one side, or the most shameless and opportunistic on the other, willingly enter. The result is a citizenry clearly disgusted with politics, politicians, and American governance in general.

But our problems are larger and deeper. To have recourse to all that has been already argued, when we begin believing that any particular right — the right to bear arms, the right to "free expression," the right to abortion, to privacy, even to speech and religion as we understand them — can brook no regulation, then the compromises necessary for democratic life become impossible. If we believe that liberty is unbounded — that rights are absolute and simply individualistic, that personal freedom trumps every other good, that our rights are the same as our interests or our desires, that moderation is a synonym for capitulation, and that true freedom means the release from all constraints, be they moral, religious, conventional, or simply historic — then we are rending the fabric of the Constitution while deluding ourselves that we are honoring it. Finally, when we absolutize our rights to privacy and personal liberty over the more general right of us all to protection against foreign enemies, then even the security and safety of the entire nation is at risk.

When we have an understanding of justice that is rigid and when we regard the means of reaching it as non-negotiable, then little remains but strife. This goes for economic justice, racial justice, ecological justice, and equality in matters of gender and lifestyle. When questioning a mandate that the public provide free contraceptives and abortifacients is condemned as waging a "war on women," when those who resist celebrating or supporting every lifestyle choice are stigmatized, when those who work honestly within the free market are told that capitalism is the source of all social evil, when well-respected political figures say that those who are skeptical of the arguments regarding climate change should be treated as "traitors" and jailed as war criminals, or — to pull these various threads together — when "No Justice No Peace" becomes the understanding of a sufficiently large segment of the population, the country is in truly serious danger.

What we see today is an America deeply in conflict over its values. On one side there's a more traditional America: patriotic, often quite religious, temperate in its habits and its expectations, proud of the country, self-reliant and hard-working, able quietly to tend to its own business yet ready to lend a hand to friends and neighbors, old-fashioned in its outlook and, because of that, upset by the character of modernity and bewildered by its excesses. It sometimes raises itself up to engage in political action; sometimes it simply falls back as it recoils from all that it sees in contemporary politics.

Another side of America is split between staunch libertarians and radical egalitarians. For their part, libertarians see attacks on liberty in almost everything that the society collectively tries to do. Any surveillance portends the coming of a police state, most attempts to restrict obscene material threaten free expression, and so forth. Some are more rabid in their views or more conspiratorial in their outlook than others, but all fail to see appreciate Madison's concern: that sometimes the greatest threat to our rights arises through the radicalization of our rights. Nor do libertarians appreciate that the Constitution doesn't rest simply on one pillar — the promotion of liberty — but on all the six pillars that the Preamble to that document mentions, including domestic tranquility and providing for the common defense. Are these six goals of political life in tension? Yes, often they are. They were in tension at the Founding and remain so today. But the task of constitutional politics, the task of *statesmanship*, is to weave all these strands together, not to glorify one and denigrate the others.

On the other hand, if you believe, as many contemporary egalitarians do, that the principle of equality demands a fundamental overhaul of the American economic system, the redistribution of wealth, the equal merit of all cultures (except ours, which is bad), or that justice necessitates equalizing power internationally rather than first emphasizing American national security and defense, then you will be part of that other America that is often so critical of the Founders, their Constitution, and the America they helped establish. And you will be undermining the fairest system of politics and economics in human history, all in the name of a radicalized and wrong view of equality and a partial and unjust understanding of the meaning of justice.

* * * * *

I began both this book and this chapter by referencing what others see when they look at our present-day regime of equal liberty. Sadly, (to paraphrase the title of an essay by the late Irving Kristol that I mentioned earlier) to many who live elsewhere, America today seems a place where liberty has lost her loveliness. A place where "rights" are increasingly seen as the opponents of traditional virtues, of religion, and even of freedom of speech and thought in their most basic forms — that is, of the open exchange of ideas and arguments without fear of being silenced by the sensitive, the progressive, or the politically correct.

Let's think about this last point regarding freedom of thought and speech one last time, since it is paradigmatic of much of what has changed for the worse in this country. Now, to be sure, if a "satirist" somewhere wishes to publish juvenile cartoons of Muhammad, perhaps along with one of a Catholic nun giving oral sex, we in the West will move heaven and earth in support of the journal's "freedom of speech." But try to have a serious discussion of Islam and its historical relation to violence and you run the risk of being accused of hate speech or be disinvited from giving the commencement speech at a "liberal" university. Try to make a point about the possible connections between culture and crime in the inner city and see how quickly accusations of "racism" get hurled. Or try to defend traditional marriage or even traditional understanding of proper human behavior and see the speed with which one gets branded a bigot and accused of promulgating hate and homophobia.

How confused we seem to have become. We believe in religious liberty, but recoil from those who take seriously traditional religious teachings. In speech, we celebrate every variety of "self-expression" — especially if it ridicules the prudish or discomfits the traditional. But the exercise of a robust and manly freedom of speech — a speech that takes ideas seriously and privileges argument over "expression" — has today fewer and fewer defenders.

Despite the fact that I have talked repeatedly in this book about how others understand us, perhaps the truly important issue is how, exactly, *do we understand ourselves*? Do we have in our society a proper respect for our heritage? Or do we misunderstand it and distort it? Do we prize independence and self-reliance? Or do we prefer the comforts of mild and providential governmental beneficence? Do we still honor those who have worked hard, invented, made, produced, and distributed — or do we prefer to think that "you didn't build that"? Do we prize freedom of thought, or only those thoughts that don't upset the sensitivities of people and classes deemed to be "protected"? Perhaps we especially like that speech that ridicules the old-fashioned and traditional or that "expression" that shows that God is truly dead, that all boundaries are dissolved, and that, now, all is allowed.

Depending on which side of those contrary positions America finds itself will tell us how true to our highest principles we, as a nation, remain.

* * * * *

> We shall not cease from exploration
> And the end of all our exploring
> Will be to arrive where we started
> And know the place for the first time.

These lines are from *Little Gidding*, the last of the poems that comprise T.S. Eliot's *Four Quartets*. It is, as many readers will remember, a poem about renewal and return. I offer those lines as thematic for what this small book has hoped to accomplish: In the midst of an increased interest in our Founding and its ideals, this volume has been an attempt to recapture the original meaning of both our Constitution and our founding ideas. We are, I believe, at a turning point in our national self-understanding perhaps as great as in the years before the Civil War, when Lincoln saw how the nationalization of slavery and, with it, the degradation of our founding principles of liberty and equality, put us in danger of becoming a different, and immeasurably worse, nation.[89]

It is becoming something of a commonplace to say that unless the people in a democracy are attached to their country, unless they see it as worthy and just, the country is in grave danger. Some have argued that unless those who help shape public opinion — and especially those who educate the young — see it as part of their mission to teach patriotism, the country will have lost its best defense. As historian Donald Kagan recently wrote, "Democracy — of all political systems, because it depends on the participation of its citizens in their own government and because it depends on their own free will to risk their lives in its defense — stands in the greatest need of an education that produces patriotism."[90]

However, any form of "preaching" patriotism will almost certainly have little effect. The way to counter those who feel called to demean the achievements of this country and undermine the natural affection we all should feel for it is not by moralizing lectures but by the clarity of our understanding and the strength of

---

[89] For perhaps the clearest, most penetrating, and most gripping and poetical restatement and defense of the basic principles of America and the Founding, see Lincoln's "Speech at Chicago, Illinois," July 10, 1858, in the Appendix, p. 224.

[90] Donald Kagan, "Democracy Requires a Patriotic Education," *The Wall Street Journal*, September 26, 2014.

our argument. That is, it has been part of the premise of this book from the start that understanding precedes affection — that patriotism built on ignorance, or on attachment to false principles, will be useless or worse.

But if we wish to inculcate a worthy patriotism — if we wish others to respect this place— where do we turn? I have no grand illusion that our arguments will do much to turn the purveyors of popular culture — sadly, the primary educators of the young these days — into thoughtful exponents of the American way. Somehow, songs about ordered liberty or films on the benefits of a regulated but free market probably won't seem all that appealing.

But there are others who can and should help. The immediate educators of the young are parents. So, this book is written in part for them, for ordinary citizens, in hopes that they might have in their minds what most of them know in their hearts — that the founding principles of this nation are just, rare, and worthy of transmission from their generation to the next.

Beyond parents, those in public service — legislators, representatives, senators, jurists, even presidents — can instruct in both their actions and their words. I hope that those who truly aim to serve will take seriously *what* the Founders hoped to accomplish, *why* they did what they did, and *how* they hoped to achieve it.

Above all, I hope this book is useful and instructive for teachers and professors. Tearing down is easy. The tendency to promote our own more contemporary notions while rejecting or even belittling ideas that went before helps us view ourselves as truly "critical" thinkers, and makes us feel better about ourselves. But maybe, just maybe, if we as teachers can take the Founding seriously and try to understand what today seems so easy to dismiss, we might learn something — something truly valuable not only for ourselves but also for our students and for our country.

It has been the grand hope of this book that rediscovering the meaning of the Founders' principles — attaching it again to the natural love that all men and women have to their families, their friends, and their country — might help set us back right. In the end, our greatest obligation as the Founders' inheritors is to see to it that we *understand* what they did, *respect* what they did, and *transmit* all that they did. And so, quoting Lincoln as we did at the start of this book, we end as we began:

> We find ourselves under the government of a system of political institutions conducing more essentially to the ends of civil and religious liberty than any of which the history of former times tells us. We, when mounting the stage of existence, found ourselves the legal inheritors of these fundamental blessings. We toiled not in the acquirement or establishment of them; they are a legacy bequeathed us by a once hardy, brave, and patriotic, but now lamented and departed, race of ancestors. Theirs was the task (and nobly they performed it) to possess themselves, and through themselves us, of this goodly land, and to uprear upon its hills and its valleys a political edifice of liberty and equal rights; 'tis ours only to transmit these — the former unprofaned by the foot of an invader, the latter undecayed by the lapse of time and untorn by usurpation — to the latest generation that fate shall permit the world to know. This task of gratitude to our fathers, justice to ourselves, duty to posterity, and love for our species in general, all imperatively require us faithfully to perform.

Appendices

The Declaration of Independence

IN CONGRESS, July 4, 1776.

The unanimous Declaration of the thirteen united States of America,

When in the Course of human events, it becomes necessary for one people to dissolve the political bands which have connected them with another, and to assume among the powers of the earth, the separate and equal station to which the Laws of Nature and of Nature's God entitle them, a decent respect to the opinions of mankind requires that they should declare the causes which impel them to the separation.

We hold these truths to be self-evident, that all men are created equal, that they are endowed by their Creator with certain unalienable Rights, that among these are Life, Liberty and the pursuit of Happiness.—That to secure these rights, Governments are instituted among Men, deriving their just powers from the consent of the governed,—That whenever any Form of Government becomes destructive of these ends, it is the Right of the People to alter or to abolish it, and to institute new Government, laying its foundation on such principles and organizing its powers in such form, as to them shall seem most likely to effect their Safety and Happiness. Prudence, indeed, will dictate that Governments long established should not be changed for light and transient causes; and accordingly all experience hath shewn, that mankind are more disposed to suffer, while evils are sufferable, than to right themselves by abolishing the forms to which they are accustomed. But when a long train of abuses and usurpations, pursuing invariably the same Object evinces a design to reduce them under absolute Despotism, it is their right, it is their duty, to throw off such Government, and to provide new Guards for their future security.—Such has been the patient sufferance of these Colonies; and such is now the necessity which constrains them to alter their former Systems of Government. The history of the present King of Great Britain is a history of repeated injuries and usurpations, all having in direct object the establishment of an absolute Tyranny over these States. To prove this, let Facts be submitted to a candid world.

He has refused his Assent to Laws, the most wholesome and necessary for the public good.

He has forbidden his Governors to pass Laws of immediate and pressing importance, unless suspended in their operation till his Assent should be obtained; and when so suspended, he has utterly neglected to attend to them.

He has refused to pass other Laws for the accommodation of large districts of people, unless those people would relinquish the right of Representation in the Legislature, a right inestimable to them and formidable to tyrants only.

He has called together legislative bodies at places unusual, uncomfortable, and distant from the depository of their public Records, for the sole purpose of fatiguing them into compliance with his measures.

He has dissolved Representative Houses repeatedly, for opposing with manly firmness his invasions on the rights of the people.

He has refused for a long time, after such dissolutions, to cause others to be elected; whereby the Legislative powers, incapable of Annihilation, have returned to the People at large for their exercise; the State remaining in the mean time exposed to all the dangers of invasion from without, and convulsions within.

He has endeavoured to prevent the population of these States; for that purpose obstructing the Laws for Naturalization of Foreigners; refusing to pass others to encourage their migrations hither, and raising the conditions of new

Appropriations of Lands.

He has obstructed the Administration of Justice, by refusing his Assent to Laws for establishing Judiciary powers.

He has made Judges dependent on his Will alone, for the tenure of their offices, and the amount and payment of their salaries.

He has erected a multitude of New Offices, and sent hither swarms of Officers to harrass our people, and eat out their substance.

He has kept among us, in times of peace, Standing Armies without the Consent of our legislatures.

He has affected to render the Military independent of and superior to the Civil power.

He has combined with others to subject us to a jurisdiction foreign to our constitution, and unacknowledged by our laws; giving his Assent to their Acts of pretended Legislation:

For Quartering large bodies of armed troops among us:

For protecting them, by a mock Trial, from punishment for any Murders which they should commit on the Inhabitants of these States:

For cutting off our Trade with all parts of the world:

For imposing Taxes on us without our Consent:

For depriving us in many cases, of the benefits of Trial by Jury:

For transporting us beyond Seas to be tried for pretended offences

For abolishing the free System of English Laws in a neighbouring Province, establishing therein an Arbitrary government, and enlarging its Boundaries so as to render it at once an example and fit instrument for introducing the same absolute rule into these Colonies:

For taking away our Charters, abolishing our most valuable Laws, and altering fundamentally the Forms of our Governments:

For suspending our own Legislatures, and declaring themselves invested with power to legislate for us in all cases whatsoever.

He has abdicated Government here, by declaring us out of his Protection and waging War against us.

He has plundered our seas, ravaged our Coasts, burnt our towns, and destroyed the lives of our people.

He is at this time transporting large Armies of foreign Mercenaries to compleat the works of death, desolation and tyranny, already begun with circumstances of Cruelty & perfidy scarcely paralleled in the most barbarous ages, and totally unworthy the Head of a civilized nation.

He has constrained our fellow Citizens taken Captive on the high Seas to bear Arms against their Country, to become the executioners of their friends and Brethren, or to fall themselves by their Hands.

He has excited domestic insurrections amongst us, and has endeavoured to bring on the inhabitants of our frontiers, the merciless Indian Savages, whose known rule of warfare, is an undistinguished destruction of all ages, sexes and conditions.

In every stage of these Oppressions We have Petitioned for Redress in the most humble terms: Our repeated Petitions have been answered only by repeated injury. A Prince whose character is thus marked by every act which may define a Tyrant, is unfit to be the ruler of a free people.

Nor have We been wanting in attentions to our Brittish brethren. We have warned them from time to time of attempts by their legislature to extend an unwarrantable jurisdiction over us. We have reminded them of the circumstances of our emigration and settlement here. We have appealed to their native justice and magnanimity, and we have conjured them by the ties of our common kindred to disavow these usurpations, which, would inevitably interrupt our connections and correspondence. They too have been deaf to the voice of justice and of consanguinity. We must, therefore, acquiesce in the necessity, which denounces our Separation, and hold them, as we hold the rest of mankind, Enemies in War, in Peace Friends.

We, therefore, the Representatives of the united States of America, in General Congress, Assembled, appealing to the Supreme Judge of the world for the rectitude of our intentions, do, in the Name, and by Authority of the good People of these Colonies, solemnly publish and declare, That these United Colonies are, and of Right ought to be Free and Independent States; that they are Absolved from all Allegiance to the British Crown, and that all political connection between them and the State of Great Britain, is and ought to be totally dissolved; and that as Free and Independent States, they have full Power to levy War, conclude Peace, contract Alliances, establish Commerce, and to do all other Acts and Things which Independent States may of right do. And for the support of this Declaration, with a firm reliance on the protection of divine Providence, we mutually pledge to each other our Lives, our Fortunes and our sacred Honor.

The Constitution of the United States

We the People of the United States, in Order to form a more perfect Union, establish Justice, insure domestic Tranquility, provide for the common defence, promote the general Welfare, and secure the Blessings of Liberty to ourselves and our Posterity, do ordain and establish this Constitution for the United States of America.

Article. I.

Section. 1.

All legislative Powers herein granted shall be vested in a Congress of the United States, which shall consist of a Senate and House of Representatives.

Section. 2.

The House of Representatives shall be composed of Members chosen every second Year by the People of the several States, and the Electors in each State shall have the Qualifications requisite for Electors of the most numerous Branch of the State Legislature.

No Person shall be a Representative who shall not have attained to the Age of twenty five Years, and been seven Years a Citizen of the United States, and who shall not, when elected, be an Inhabitant of that State in which he shall be chosen.

Representatives and direct Taxes shall be apportioned among the several States which may be included within this Union, according to their respective Numbers, which shall be determined by adding to the whole Number of free Persons, including those bound to Service for a Term of Years, and excluding Indians not taxed, three fifths of all other Persons. The actual Enumeration shall be made within three Years after the first Meeting of the Congress of the United States, and within every subsequent Term of ten Years, in such Manner as they shall by Law direct. The Number of Representatives shall not exceed one for every thirty Thousand, but each State shall have at Least one Representative; and until such enumeration shall be made, the State of New Hampshire shall be entitled to chuse three, Massachusetts eight, Rhode-Island and Providence Plantations one, Connecticut five, New-York six, New Jersey four, Pennsylvania eight, Delaware one, Maryland six, Virginia ten, North Carolina five, South Carolina five, and Georgia three.

When vacancies happen in the Representation from any State, the Executive Authority thereof shall issue Writs of Election to fill such Vacancies.

The House of Representatives shall chuse their Speaker and other Officers; and shall have the sole Power of Impeachment.

Section. 3.

The Senate of the United States shall be composed of two Senators from each State, chosen by the Legislature thereof, for six Years; and each Senator shall have one Vote.

Immediately after they shall be assembled in Consequence of the first Election, they shall be divided as equally as may be into three Classes. The Seats of the Senators of the first Class shall be vacated at the Expiration of the second Year, of the second Class at the Expiration of the fourth Year, and of the third Class at the Expiration of the sixth Year, so that one third may be chosen every second Year; and if Vacancies happen by Resignation, or otherwise, during the Recess of the Legislature of any State, the Executive thereof may make temporary Appointments until the next Meeting of the Legislature, which shall then fill such Vacancies.

No Person shall be a Senator who shall not have attained to the Age of thirty Years, and been nine Years a Citizen of the United States, and who shall not, when elected, be an Inhabitant of that State for which he shall be chosen.

The Vice President of the United States shall be President of the Senate, but shall have no Vote, unless they be equally divided.

The Senate shall chuse their other Officers, and also a President pro tempore, in the Absence of the Vice President, or when he shall exercise the Office of President of the United States.

The Senate shall have the sole Power to try all Impeachments. When sitting for that Purpose, they shall be on Oath or Affirmation. When the President of the United States is tried, the Chief Justice shall preside: And no Person shall be convicted without the Concurrence of two thirds of the Members present.

Judgment in Cases of Impeachment shall not extend further than to removal from Office, and disqualification to hold and enjoy any Office of honor, Trust or Profit under the United States: but the Party convicted shall nevertheless be liable and subject to Indictment, Trial, Judgment and Punishment, according to Law.

Section. 4.

The Times, Places and Manner of holding Elections for Senators and Representatives, shall be prescribed in each State by the Legislature thereof; but the Congress may at any time by Law make or alter such Regulations, except as to the Places of chusing Senators.

The Congress shall assemble at least once in every Year, and such Meeting shall be on the first Monday in December, unless they shall by Law appoint a different Day.

Section. 5.

Each House shall be the Judge of the Elections, Returns and Qualifications of its own Members, and a Majority of each shall constitute a Quorum to do Business; but a smaller Number may adjourn from day to day, and may be authorized to compel the Attendance of absent Members, in such Manner, and under such Penalties as each House may provide.

Each House may determine the Rules of its Proceedings, punish its Members for disorderly Behaviour, and, with the Concurrence of two thirds, expel a Member.

Each House shall keep a Journal of its Proceedings, and from time to time publish the same, excepting such Parts as may in their Judgment require Secrecy; and the Yeas and Nays of the Members of either House on any question shall, at the Desire of one fifth of those Present, be entered on the Journal.

Neither House, during the Session of Congress, shall, without the Consent of the other, adjourn for more than three days, nor to any other Place than that in which the two Houses shall be sitting.

Section. 6.

The Senators and Representatives shall receive a Compensation for their Services, to be ascertained by Law, and paid out of the Treasury of the United States. They shall in all Cases, except Treason, Felony and Breach of the Peace, be privileged from Arrest during their Attendance at the Session of their respective Houses, and in going to and returning from the same; and for any Speech or Debate in either House, they shall not be questioned in any other Place.

No Senator or Representative shall, during the Time for which he was elected, be appointed to any civil Office under the Authority of the United States, which shall have been created, or the Emoluments whereof shall have been encreased during such time; and no Person holding any Office under the United States, shall be a Member of either House during his Continuance in Office.

Section. 7.

All Bills for raising Revenue shall originate in the House of Representatives; but the Senate may propose or concur with Amendments as on other Bills.

Every Bill which shall have passed the House of Representatives and the Senate, shall, before it become a Law, be presented to the President of the United States; If he approve he shall sign it, but if not he shall return it, with his Objections to that House in which it shall have originated, who shall enter the Objections at large on their Journal, and proceed to reconsider it. If after such Reconsideration two thirds of that House shall agree to pass the Bill, it shall be sent, together with the Objections, to the other House, by which it shall likewise be reconsidered, and if approved by two thirds of that House, it shall become a Law. But in all such Cases the Votes of both Houses shall be determined by yeas and Nays, and the Names of the Persons voting for and against the Bill shall be entered on the Journal of each House respectively. If any Bill shall not be returned by the President within ten Days (Sundays excepted) after it shall have been presented to him, the Same shall be a Law, in like Manner as if he had signed it, unless the Congress by their Adjournment prevent its Return, in which Case it shall not be a Law.

Every Order, Resolution, or Vote to which the Concurrence of the Senate and House of Representatives may be necessary (except on a question of Adjournment) shall be presented to the President of the United States; and before the Same shall take Effect, shall be approved by him, or being disapproved by him, shall be repassed by two thirds of the Senate and House of Representatives, according to the Rules and Limitations prescribed in the Case of a Bill.

Section. 8.

The Congress shall have Power To lay and collect Taxes, Duties, Imposts and Excises, to pay the Debts and provide for the common Defence and general Welfare of the United States; but all Duties, Imposts and Excises shall be uniform throughout the United States;

To borrow Money on the credit of the United States;

To regulate Commerce with foreign Nations, and among the several States, and with the Indian Tribes;

To establish an uniform Rule of Naturalization, and uniform Laws on the subject of Bankruptcies throughout the United States;

To coin Money, regulate the Value thereof, and of foreign Coin, and fix the Standard of Weights and Measures;

To provide for the Punishment of counterfeiting the Securities and current Coin of the United States;

To establish Post Offices and post Roads;

To promote the Progress of Science and useful Arts, by securing for limited Times to Authors and Inventors the exclusive Right to their respective Writings and Discoveries;

To constitute Tribunals inferior to the supreme Court;

To define and punish Piracies and Felonies committed on the high Seas, and Offences against the Law of Nations;

To declare War, grant Letters of Marque and Reprisal, and make Rules concerning Captures on Land and Water;

To raise and support Armies, but no Appropriation of Money to that Use shall be for a longer Term than two Years;

To provide and maintain a Navy;

To make Rules for the Government and Regulation of the land and naval Forces;

To provide for calling forth the Militia to execute the Laws of the Union, suppress Insurrections and repel Invasions;

To provide for organizing, arming, and disciplining, the Militia, and for governing such Part of them as may be employed in the Service of the United States, reserving to the States respectively, the Appointment of the Officers, and the Authority of training the Militia according to the discipline prescribed by Congress;

To exercise exclusive Legislation in all Cases whatsoever, over such District (not exceeding ten Miles square) as may, by Cession of particular States, and the Acceptance of Congress, become the Seat of the Government of the United States, and to exercise like Authority over all Places purchased by the Consent of the Legislature of the State in which the Same shall be, for the Erection of Forts, Magazines, Arsenals, dock-Yards, and other needful Buildings;— And

To make all Laws which shall be necessary and proper for carrying into Execution the foregoing Powers, and all other Powers vested by this Constitution in the Government of the United States, or in any Department or Officer thereof.

Section. 9.

The Migration or Importation of such Persons as any of the States now existing shall think proper to admit, shall not be prohibited by the Congress prior to the Year one thousand eight hundred and eight, but a Tax or duty may be imposed on such Importation, not exceeding ten dollars for each Person.

The Privilege of the Writ of Habeas Corpus shall not be

suspended, unless when in Cases of Rebellion or Invasion the public Safety may require it.

No Bill of Attainder or ex post facto Law shall be passed.

No Capitation, or other direct, Tax shall be laid, unless in Proportion to the Census or enumeration herein before directed to be taken.

No Tax or Duty shall be laid on Articles exported from any State.

No Preference shall be given by any Regulation of Commerce or Revenue to the Ports of one State over those of another: nor shall Vessels bound to, or from, one State, be obliged to enter, clear, or pay Duties in another.

No Money shall be drawn from the Treasury, but in Consequence of Appropriations made by Law; and a regular Statement and Account of the Receipts and Expenditures of all public Money shall be published from time to time.

No Title of Nobility shall be granted by the United States: And no Person holding any Office of Profit or Trust under them, shall, without the Consent of the Congress, accept of any present, Emolument, Office, or Title, of any kind whatever, from any King, Prince, or foreign State.

Section. 10.

No State shall enter into any Treaty, Alliance, or Confederation; grant Letters of Marque and Reprisal; coin Money; emit Bills of Credit; make any Thing but gold and silver Coin a Tender in Payment of Debts; pass any Bill of Attainder, ex post facto Law, or Law impairing the Obligation of Contracts, or grant any Title of Nobility.

No State shall, without the Consent of the Congress, lay any Imposts or Duties on Imports or Exports, except what may be absolutely necessary for executing it's inspection

Laws: and the net Produce of all Duties and Imposts, laid by any State on Imports or Exports, shall be for the Use of the Treasury of the United States; and all such Laws shall be subject to the Revision and Controul of the Congress.

No State shall, without the Consent of Congress, lay any Duty of Tonnage, keep Troops, or Ships of War in time of Peace, enter into any Agreement or Compact with another State, or with a foreign Power, or engage in War, unless actually invaded, or in such imminent Danger as will not admit of delay.

Article. II.

Section. 1.

The executive Power shall be vested in a President of the United States of America. He shall hold his Office during the Term of four Years, and, together with the Vice President, chosen for the same Term, be elected, as follows

Each State shall appoint, in such Manner as the Legislature thereof may direct, a Number of Electors, equal to the whole Number of Senators and Representatives to which the State may be entitled in the Congress: but no Senator or Representative, or Person holding an Office of Trust or Profit under the United States, shall be appointed an Elector.

The Electors shall meet in their respective States, and vote by Ballot for two Persons, of whom one at least shall not be an Inhabitant of the same State with themselves. And they shall make a List of all the Persons voted for, and of the Number of Votes for each; which List they shall sign and certify, and transmit sealed to the Seat of the Government of the United States, directed to the President of the Senate. The President of the Senate shall, in the Presence of the Senate and House of Representatives, open all the Certificates, and the Votes shall then be counted. The Person having the greatest Number of Votes shall be the President, if such Number be a Majority of the whole Number of Electors appointed; and if there be more than one who have such Majority, and have an equal Number of Votes, then the House of Representatives shall immediately chuse by Ballot one of them for President; and if no Person have a Majority, then from the five highest on the List the said House shall in like Manner chuse the President. But in chusing the President, the Votes shall be taken by States, the Representation from each State having one Vote; A quorum for this Purpose shall consist of a Member or Members from two thirds of the States, and a Majority of all the States shall be necessary to a Choice. In every Case, after the Choice of the President, the Person having the greatest Number of Votes of the Electors shall be the Vice President. But if there should remain two or more who have equal Votes, the Senate shall chuse from them by Ballot the Vice President.

The Congress may determine the Time of chusing the Electors, and the Day on which they shall give their Votes; which Day shall be the same throughout the United States.

No Person except a natural born Citizen, or a Citizen of the United States, at the time of the Adoption of this Constitution, shall be eligible to the Office of President; neither shall any Person be eligible to that Office who shall not have attained to the Age of thirty five Years, and been fourteen Years a Resident within the United States.

In Case of the Removal of the President from Office, or of his Death, Resignation, or Inability to discharge the Powers and Duties of the said Office, the Same shall devolve on the Vice President, and the Congress may by Law provide for the Case of Removal, Death, Resignation or Inability, both of the President and Vice President, declaring what Officer shall then act as President, and such Officer shall act accordingly, until the Disability be removed, or a President shall be elected.

The President shall, at stated Times, receive for his Services, a Compensation, which shall neither be encreased nor diminished during the Period for which he shall have been elected, and he shall not receive within that Period any other Emolument from the United States, or any of them.

Before hc enter on the Execution of his Office, he shall take the following Oath or Affirmation:—"I do solemnly swear (or affirm) that I will faithfully execute the Office of President of the United States, and will to the best of my Ability, preserve, protect and defend the Constitution of the United States."

Section. 2.

The President shall be Commander in Chief of the Army and Navy of the United States, and of the Militia of the several States, when called into the actual Service of the United States; he may require the Opinion, in writing, of the principal Officer in each of the executive Departments, upon any Subject relating to the Duties of their respective Offices, and he shall have Power to grant Reprieves and Pardons for Offences against the United States, except in Cases of Impeachment.

He shall have Power, by and with the Advice and Consent of the Senate, to make Treaties, provided two thirds of the Senators present concur; and he shall nominate, and by and with the Advice and Consent of the Senate, shall appoint Ambassadors, other public Ministers and Consuls, Judges of the supreme Court, and all other Officers of the United States, whose Appointments are not herein otherwise provided for, and which shall be established by Law: but the Congress may by Law vest the Appointment of such inferior Officers, as they think proper, in the President alone, in the Courts of Law, or in the Heads of Departments.

The President shall have Power to fill up all Vacancies that may happen during the Recess of the Senate, by granting Commissions which shall expire at the End of their next

Session.

Section. 3.

He shall from time to time give to the Congress Information of the State of the Union, and recommend to their Consideration such Measures as he shall judge necessary and expedient; he may, on extraordinary Occasions, convene both Houses, or either of them, and in Case of Disagreement between them, with Respect to the Time of Adjournment, he may adjourn them to such Time as he shall think proper; he shall receive Ambassadors and other public Ministers; he shall take Care that the Laws be faithfully executed, and shall Commission all the Officers of the United States.

Section. 4.

The President, Vice President and all civil Officers of the United States, shall be removed from Office on Impeachment for, and Conviction of, Treason, Bribery, or other high Crimes and Misdemeanors.

Article III.

Section. 1.

The judicial Power of the United States, shall be vested in one supreme Court, and in such inferior Courts as the Congress may from time to time ordain and establish. The Judges, both of the supreme and inferior Courts, shall hold their Offices during good Behaviour, and shall, at stated Times, receive for their Services, a Compensation, which shall not be diminished during their Continuance in Office.

Section. 2.

The judicial Power shall extend to all Cases, in Law and Equity, arising under this Constitution, the Laws of the United States, and Treaties made, or which shall be made, under their Authority;—to all Cases affecting Ambassadors, other public Ministers and Consuls;—to all Cases of admiralty and maritime Jurisdiction;—to Controversies to which the United States shall be a Party;—to Controversies between two or more States;—between a State and Citizens of another State,—between Citizens of different States,—between Citizens of the same State claiming Lands under Grants of different States, and between a State, or the Citizens thereof, and foreign States, Citizens or Subjects.

In all Cases affecting Ambassadors, other public Ministers and Consuls, and those in which a State shall be Party, the supreme Court shall have original Jurisdiction. In all the other Cases before mentioned, the supreme Court shall have appellate Jurisdiction, both as to Law and Fact, with such Exceptions, and under such Regulations as the Congress shall make.

The Trial of all Crimes, except in Cases of Impeachment, shall be by Jury; and such Trial shall be held in the State where the said Crimes shall have been committed; but when not committed within any State, the Trial shall be at such Place or Places as the Congress may by Law have directed.

Section. 3.

Treason against the United States, shall consist only in levying War against them, or in adhering to their Enemies, giving them Aid and Comfort. No Person shall be convicted of Treason unless on the Testimony of two Witnesses to the same overt Act, or on Confession in open Court.

The Congress shall have Power to declare the Punishment of Treason, but no Attainder of Treason shall work Corruption of Blood, or Forfeiture except during the Life of the Person attainted.

Article. IV.

Section. 1.

Full Faith and Credit shall be given in each State to the public Acts, Records, and judicial Proceedings of every other State. And the Congress may by general Laws prescribe the Manner in which such Acts, Records and Proceedings shall be proved, and the Effect thereof.

Section. 2.

The Citizens of each State shall be entitled to all Privileges and Immunities of Citizens in the several States.

A Person charged in any State with Treason, Felony, or other Crime, who shall flee from Justice, and be found in another State, shall on Demand of the executive Authority of the State from which he fled, be delivered up, to be removed to the State having Jurisdiction of the Crime.

No Person held to Service or Labour in one State, under the Laws thereof, escaping into another, shall, in Consequence of any Law or Regulation therein, be discharged from such Service or Labour, but shall be delivered up on Claim of the Party to whom such Service or Labour may be due.

Section. 3.

New States may be admitted by the Congress into this Union; but no new State shall be formed or erected within the Jurisdiction of any other State; nor any State be formed by the Junction of two or more States, or Parts of States, without the Consent of the Legislatures of the States concerned as well as of the Congress.

The Congress shall have Power to dispose of and make all needful Rules and Regulations respecting the Territory or other Property belonging to the United States; and nothing in this Constitution shall be so construed as to Prejudice any Claims of the United States, or of any particular State.

Section. 4.

The United States shall guarantee to every State in this Union a Republican Form of Government, and shall protect each of them against Invasion; and on Application of the Legislature, or of the Executive (when the Legislature cannot be convened), against domestic Violence.

Article. V.

The Congress, whenever two thirds of both Houses shall deem it necessary, shall propose Amendments to this Constitution, or, on the Application of the Legislatures of two thirds of the several States, shall call a Convention for proposing Amendments, which, in either Case, shall be valid to all Intents and Purposes, as Part of this Constitution, when ratified by the Legislatures of three fourths of the several States, or by Conventions in three fourths thereof, as the one or the other Mode of Ratification may be proposed by the Congress; Provided that no Amendment which may be made prior to the Year One thousand eight hundred and eight shall in any Manner affect the first and fourth Clauses in the Ninth Section of the first Article; and that no State, without its Consent, shall be deprived of its equal Suffrage in the Senate.

Article. VI.

All Debts contracted and Engagements entered into, before the Adoption of this Constitution, shall be as valid against the United States under this Constitution, as under the Confederation.

This Constitution, and the Laws of the United States which shall be made in Pursuance thereof; and all Treaties made, or which shall be made, under the Authority of the United States, shall be the supreme Law of the Land; and the Judges in every State shall be bound thereby, any Thing in the Constitution or Laws of any State to the Contrary notwithstanding.

The Senators and Representatives before mentioned, and the Members of the several State Legislatures, and all executive and judicial Officers, both of the United States and of the several States, shall be bound by Oath or Affirmation, to support this Constitution; but no religious Test shall ever be required as a Qualification to any Office or public Trust under the United States.

Article. VII.

The Ratification of the Conventions of nine States, shall be sufficient for the Establishment of this Constitution between the States so ratifying the Same.

Attest William Jackson Secretary

Done in Convention by the Unanimous Consent of the States present the Seventeenth Day of September in the Year of our Lord one thousand seven hundred and Eighty seven and of the Independance of the United States of America the Twelfth In witness whereof We have hereunto subscribed our Names,

G°. Washington
Presidt and deputy from Virginia

Delaware
Geo: Read
Gunning Bedford jun
John Dickinson
Richard Bassett
Jaco: Broom

Maryland
James McHenry
Dan of St Thos. Jenifer
Danl. Carroll

Virginia
John Blair

James Madison Jr.

North Carolina
Wm. Blount
Richd. Dobbs Spaight
Hu Williamson

South Carolina
J. Rutledge
Charles Cotesworth Pinckney
Charles Pinckney
Pierce Butler

Georgia
William Few
Abr Baldwin

New Hampshire
John Langdon
Nicholas Gilman

Massachusetts
Nathaniel Gorham
Rufus King

Connecticut
Wm. Saml. Johnson
Roger Sherman

New York
Alexander Hamilton

New Jersey
Wil: Livingston
David Brearley
Wm. Paterson
Jona: Dayton

Pensylvania
B Franklin

Thomas Mifflin
Robt. Morris
Geo. Clymer
Thos. FitzSimons
Jared Ingersoll
James Wilson
Gouv Morris

Bill of Rights: Amendments I-X

Amendment I

Congress shall make no law respecting an establishment of religion, or prohibiting the free exercise thereof; or abridging the freedom of speech, or of the press; or the right of the people peaceably to assemble, and to petition the Government for a redress of grievances.

Amendment II

A well regulated Militia, being necessary to the security of a free State, the right of the people to keep and bear Arms, shall not be infringed.

Amendment III

No Soldier shall, in time of peace be quartered in any house, without the consent of the Owner, nor in time of war, but in a manner to be prescribed by law.

Amendment IV

The right of the people to be secure in their persons, houses, papers, and effects, against unreasonable searches and seizures, shall not be violated, and no Warrants shall issue, but upon probable cause, supported by Oath or affirmation, and particularly describing the place to be searched, and the persons or things to be seized.

Amendment V

No person shall be held to answer for a capital, or otherwise infamous crime, unless on a presentment or indictment of a Grand Jury, except in cases arising in the land or naval forces, or in the Militia, when in actual service in time of War or public danger; nor shall any person be subject for the same offence to be twice put in jeopardy of life or limb; nor shall be compelled in any criminal case to be a witness against himself, nor be deprived of life, liberty, or property, without due process of law; nor shall private property be taken for public use, without just compensation.

Amendment VI

In all criminal prosecutions, the accused shall enjoy the right to a speedy and public trial, by an impartial jury of the State and district wherein the crime shall have been committed, which district shall have been previously ascertained by law, and to be informed of the nature and cause of the accusation; to be confronted with the witnesses against him; to have compulsory process for obtaining witnesses in his favor, and to have the Assistance of Counsel for his defence.

Amendment VII

In Suits at common law, where the value in controversy shall exceed twenty dollars, the right of trial by jury shall be preserved, and no fact tried by a jury, shall be otherwise re-examined in any Court of the United States, than according to the rules of the common law.

Amendment VIII

Excessive bail shall not be required, nor excessive fines imposed, nor cruel and unusual punishments inflicted.

Amendment IX

The enumeration in the Constitution, of certain rights, shall not be construed to deny or disparage others retained by the people.

Amendment X

The powers not delegated to the United States by the Constitution, nor prohibited by it to the States, are reserved to the States respectively, or to the people.

Amendments XI-XXVII

Amendment XI

The Judicial power of the United States shall not be construed to extend to any suit in law or equity, commenced or prosecuted against one of the United States by Citizens of another State, or by Citizens or Subjects of any Foreign State.

Amendment XII

The Electors shall meet in their respective states and vote by ballot for President and Vice-President, one of whom, at least, shall not be an inhabitant of the same state with themselves; they shall name in their ballots the person voted for as President, and in distinct ballots the person voted for as Vice-President, and they shall make distinct lists of all persons voted for as President, and of all persons voted for as Vice-President, and of the number of votes for each, which lists they shall sign and certify, and transmit sealed to the seat of the government of the United States, directed to the President of the Senate; — the President of the Senate shall, in the presence of the Senate and House of Representatives, open all the certificates and the votes shall then be counted; — The person having the greatest number of votes for President, shall be the President, if such number be a majority of the whole number of Electors appointed; and if no person have such majority, then from the persons having the highest numbers not exceeding three on the list of those voted for as President, the House of Representatives shall choose immediately, by ballot, the President. But in choosing the President, the votes shall be taken by states, the representation from each state having one vote; a quorum for this purpose shall consist of a member or members from two-thirds of the states, and a majority of all the states shall be necessary to a choice. And if the House of Representatives shall not choose a President whenever the right of choice shall devolve upon them, before the fourth day of March next following, then the Vice-President shall act as President, as in case of the death or other constitutional disability of the President. — The person having the greatest number of votes as Vice-President, shall be the Vice-President, if such number be a majority of the whole number of Electors appointed, and if no person have a majority, then from the two highest numbers on the list, the Senate shall choose the Vice-President; a quorum for the purpose shall consist of two-thirds of the whole number of Senators, and a majority of the whole number shall be necessary to a choice. But no person constitutionally ineligible to the office of President shall be eligible to that of Vice-President of the United States.

Amendment XIII

Section 1.

Neither slavery nor involuntary servitude, except as a punishment for crime whereof the party shall have been duly convicted, shall exist within the United States, or any place subject to their jurisdiction.

Section 2.

Congress shall have power to enforce this article by appropriate legislation.

Amendment XIV

Section 1.

All persons born or naturalized in the United States, and subject to the jurisdiction thereof, are citizens of the United States and of the State wherein they reside. No State shall make or enforce any law which shall abridge the privileges or immunities of citizens of the United States; nor shall any State deprive any person of life, liberty, or property, without due process of law; nor deny to any person within its jurisdiction the equal protection of the laws.

Section 2.

Representatives shall be apportioned among the several States according to their respective numbers, counting the whole number of persons in each State, excluding Indians not taxed. But when the right to vote at any election for the choice of electors for President and Vice-President of the United States, Representatives in Congress, the Executive and Judicial officers of a State, or the members of the Legislature thereof, is denied to any of the male inhabitants of such State, being twenty-one years of age, and citizens of the United States, or in any way abridged, except for participation in rebellion, or other crime, the basis of representation therein shall be reduced in the proportion which the number of such male citizens shall bear to the whole number of male citizens twenty-one years of age in such State.

Section 3.

No person shall be a Senator or Representative in Congress, or elector of President and Vice-President, or hold any office, civil or military, under the United States, or under any State, who, having previously taken an oath, as a member of Congress, or as an officer of the United States, or as a member of any State legislature, or as an executive or judicial officer of any State, to support the Constitution of the United States, shall have engaged in insurrection or rebellion against the same, or given aid or comfort to the enemies thereof. But Congress may by a vote of two-thirds of each House, remove such disability.

Section 4.

The validity of the public debt of the United States, authorized by law, including debts incurred for payment of pensions and bounties for services in suppressing insurrection or rebellion, shall not be questioned. But neither the United States nor any State shall assume or pay any debt or obligation incurred in aid of insurrection or rebellion against the United States, or any claim for the loss or emancipation of any slave; but all such debts, obligations and claims shall be held illegal and void.

Section 5.

The Congress shall have the power to enforce, by appropriate legislation, the provisions of this article.

Amendment XV

Section 1.

The right of citizens of the United States to vote shall not be denied or abridged by the United States or by any State on account of race, color, or previous condition of servitude—

Section 2.

The Congress shall have the power to enforce this article by appropriate legislation.

Amendment XVI

The Congress shall have power to lay and collect taxes on incomes, from whatever source derived, without apportionment among the several States, and without regard to any census or enumeration.

Amendment XVII

The Senate of the United States shall be composed of two Senators from each State, elected by the people thereof, for six years; and each Senator shall have one vote. The electors in each State shall have the qualifications requisite for electors of the most numerous branch of the State legislatures.

When vacancies happen in the representation of any State in the Senate, the executive authority of such State shall issue writs of election to fill such vacancies: Provided, That the legislature of any State may empower the executive thereof to make temporary appointments until the people fill the vacancies by election as the legislature may direct.

This amendment shall not be so construed as to affect the election or term of any Senator chosen before it becomes valid as part of the Constitution.

Amendment XVIII

Section 1.

After one year from the ratification of this article the manufacture, sale, or transportation of intoxicating liquors within, the importation thereof into, or the exportation thereof from the United States and all territory subject to the jurisdiction thereof for beverage purposes is hereby prohibited.

Section 2.

The Congress and the several States shall have concurrent power to enforce this article by appropriate legislation.

Section 3.

This article shall be inoperative unless it shall have been ratified as an amendment to the Constitution by the legislatures of the several States, as provided in the Constitution, within seven years from the date of the submission hereof to the States by the Congress.

Amendment XIX

The right of citizens of the United States to vote shall not be denied or abridged by the United States or by any State on account of sex.

Congress shall have power to enforce this article by appropriate legislation.

Amendment XX

Section 1.

The terms of the President and the Vice President shall end at noon on the 20th day of January, and the terms of Senators and Representatives at noon on the 3d day of January, of the years in which such terms would have ended if this article had not been ratified; and the terms of their successors shall then begin.

Section 2.

The Congress shall assemble at least once in every year, and such meeting shall begin at noon on the 3d day of January, unless they shall by law appoint a different day.

Section 3.

If, at the time fixed for the beginning of the term of the President, the President elect shall have died, the Vice President elect shall become President. If a President shall not have been chosen before the time fixed for the beginning of his term, or if the President elect shall have failed to qualify, then the Vice President elect shall act as President until a President shall have qualified; and the Congress may by law provide for the case wherein neither a President elect nor a Vice President elect shall have qualified, declaring who shall then act as President, or the manner in which one who is to act shall be selected, and such person shall act accordingly until a President or Vice President shall have qualified.

Section 4.

The Congress may by law provide for the case of the death of any of the persons from whom the House of Representatives may choose a President whenever the right of choice shall have devolved upon them, and for the case of the death of any of the persons from whom the Senate may choose a Vice President whenever the right of choice shall have devolved upon them.

Section 5.

Sections 1 and 2 shall take effect on the 15th day of October following the ratification of this article.

Section 6.

This article shall be inoperative unless it shall have been ratified as an amendment to the Constitution by the legislatures of three-fourths of the several States within seven years from the date of its submission.

Amendment XXI

Section 1.

The eighteenth article of amendment to the Constitution of the United States is hereby repealed.

Section 2.

The transportation or importation into any State, Territory, or possession of the United States for delivery or use therein of intoxicating liquors, in violation of the laws thereof, is hereby prohibited.

Section 3.

This article shall be inoperative unless it shall have been ratified as an amendment to the Constitution by conventions in the several States, as provided in the Constitution, within seven years from the date of the submission hereof to the States by the Congress.

Amendment XXII

Section 1.

No person shall be elected to the office of the President more than twice, and no person who has held the office of President, or acted as President, for more than two years of a term to which some other person was elected President shall be elected to the office of the President more than once. But this Article shall not apply to any person holding the office of President when this Article was proposed by the Congress, and shall not prevent any person who may be holding the office of President, or acting as President, during the term within which this Article becomes operative from holding the office of President or acting as President during the remainder of such term.

Section 2.

This article shall be inoperative unless it shall have been ratified as an amendment to the Constitution by the legislatures of three-fourths of the several States within seven years from the date of its submission to the States by the Congress.

Amendment XXIII

Section 1.

The District constituting the seat of Government of the United States shall appoint in such manner as the Congress may direct:

A number of electors of President and Vice President equal to the whole number of Senators and Representatives in Congress to which the District would be entitled if it were a State, but in no event more than the least populous State; they shall be in addition to those appointed by the States, but they shall be considered, for the purposes of the election of President and Vice President, to be electors appointed by a State; and they shall meet in the District and perform such duties as provided by the twelfth article of amendment.

Section 2.

The Congress shall have power to enforce this article by appropriate legislation.

Amendment XXIV

Section 1.

The right of citizens of the United States to vote in any primary or other election for President or Vice President, for electors for President or Vice President, or for Senator or Representative in Congress, shall not be denied or abridged by the United States or any State by reason of failure to pay any poll tax or other tax.

Section 2.

The Congress shall have power to enforce this article by appropriate legislation.

Amendment XXV

Section 1.

In case of the removal of the President from office or of his death or resignation, the Vice President shall become President.

Section 2.

Whenever there is a vacancy in the office of the Vice President, the President shall nominate a Vice President who shall take office upon confirmation by a majority vote of both Houses of Congress.

Section 3.

Whenever the President transmits to the President pro tempore of the Senate and the Speaker of the House of Representatives his written declaration that he is unable to discharge the powers and duties of his office, and until he transmits to them a written declaration to the contrary, such powers and duties shall be discharged by the Vice President as Acting President.

Section 4.

Whenever the Vice President and a majority of either the principal officers of the executive departments or of such other body as Congress may by law provide, transmit to the President pro tempore of the Senate and the Speaker of the House of Representatives their written declaration that the President is unable to discharge the powers and duties of his office, the Vice President shall immediately assume the powers and duties of the office as Acting President.

Thereafter, when the President transmits to the President pro tempore of the Senate and the Speaker of the House of Representatives his written declaration that no inability exists, he shall resume the powers and duties of his office unless the Vice President and a majority of either the principal officers of the executive department or of such other body as Congress may by law provide, transmit within four days to the President pro tempore of the Senate and the

Speaker of the House of Representatives their written declaration that the President is unable to discharge the powers and duties of his office. Thereupon Congress shall decide the issue, assembling within forty-eight hours for that purpose if not in session. If the Congress, within twenty-one days after receipt of the latter written declaration, or, if Congress is not in session, within twenty-one days after Congress is required to assemble, determines by two-thirds vote of both Houses that the President is unable to discharge the powers and duties of his office, the Vice President shall continue to discharge the same as Acting President; otherwise, the President shall resume the powers and duties of his office.

Amendment XXVI

Section 1.

The right of citizens of the United States, who are eighteen years of age or older, to vote shall not be denied or abridged by the United States or by any State on account of age.

Section 2.

The Congress shall have power to enforce this article by appropriate legislation.

Amendment XXVII

No law, varying the compensation for the services of the Senators and Representatives, shall take effect, until an election of Representatives shall have intervened.

The Federalist Papers

No. 1
Alexander Hamilton

To the People of the State of New York:

AFTER an unequivocal experience of the inefficiency of the subsisting federal government, you are called upon to deliberate on a new Constitution for the United States of America. The subject speaks its own importance; comprehending in its consequences nothing less than the existence of the UNION, the safety and welfare of the parts of which it is composed, the fate of an empire in many respects the most interesting in the world. It has been frequently remarked that it seems to have been reserved to the people of this country, by their conduct and example, to decide the important question, whether societies of men are really capable or not of establishing good government from reflection and choice, or whether they are forever destined to depend for their political constitutions on accident and force. If there be any truth in the remark, the crisis at which we are arrived may with propriety be regarded as the era in which that decision is to be made; and a wrong election of the part we shall act may, in this view, deserve to be considered as the general misfortune of mankind.

This idea will add the inducements of philanthropy to those of patriotism, to heighten the solicitude which all considerate and good men must feel for the event. Happy will it be if our choice should be directed by a judicious estimate of our true interests, unperplexed and unbiased by considerations not connected with the public good. But this is a thing more ardently to be wished than seriously to be expected. The plan offered to our deliberations affects too many particular interests, innovates upon too many local institutions, not to involve in its discussion a variety of objects foreign to its merits, and of views, passions and prejudices little favorable to the discovery of truth.

Among the most formidable of the obstacles which the new Constitution will have to encounter may readily be distinguished the obvious interest of a certain class of men in every State to resist all changes which may hazard a diminution of the power, emolument, and consequence of the offices they hold under the State establishments; and the perverted ambition of another class of men, who will either hope to aggrandize themselves by the confusions of their country, or will flatter themselves with fairer prospects of elevation from the subdivision of the empire into several partial confederacies than from its union under one government.

It is not, however, my design to dwell upon observations of this nature. I am well aware that it would be disingenuous to resolve indiscriminately the opposition of any set of men (merely because their situations might subject them to suspicion) into interested or ambitious views. Candor will oblige us to admit that even such men may be actuated by upright intentions; and it cannot be doubted that much of the opposition which has made its appearance, or may hereafter make its appearance, will spring from sources, blameless at least, if not respectable—the honest errors of minds led astray by preconceived jealousies and fears. So numerous indeed and so powerful are the causes which serve to give a false bias to the judgment, that we, upon many occasions, see wise and good men on the wrong as well as on the right side of questions of the first magnitude to society. This circumstance, if duly attended to, would furnish a lesson of moderation to those who are ever so much persuaded of their being in the right in any controversy. And a further reason for caution, in this respect, might be drawn from the reflection that we are not always sure that those who advocate the truth are influenced by purer principles than their antagonists. Ambition, avarice, personal animosity, party opposition, and many other motives not more laudable than these, are apt to operate as well upon those who support as those who oppose the right side of a question. Were there not even these inducements to moderation, nothing could be more ill-judged than that intolerant spirit which has, at all times, characterized political parties. For in politics, as in religion, it is equally absurd to aim at making proselytes by fire and sword. Heresies in either can rarely be cured by persecution.

And yet, however just these sentiments will be allowed to be, we have already sufficient indications that it will happen in this as in all former cases of great national discussion. A torrent of angry and malignant passions will be let loose. To judge from the conduct of the opposite parties, we shall be led to conclude that they will mutually hope to evince the justness of their opinions, and to increase the number of their converts by the loudness of their declamations and the bitterness of their invectives. An enlightened zeal for the energy and efficiency of government will be stigmatized as the offspring of a temper fond of despotic power and hostile to the principles of liberty. An over-scrupulous jealousy of danger to the rights of the people, which is more commonly the fault of the head than of the heart, will be represented as mere pretense and artifice, the stale bait for popularity at the expense of the public good. It will be forgotten, on the one hand, that jealousy is the usual concomitant of love, and that the noble enthusiasm of liberty is apt to be infected with a spirit of narrow and illiberal distrust. On the other hand, it will be equally forgotten that the vigor of government is essential to the security of liberty; that, in the contemplation of a sound and well-informed judgment, their interest can never be separated; and that a dangerous ambition more often lurks behind the specious mask of zeal for the rights of the people than under the forbidden appearance of zeal for the firmness and efficiency of government. History will teach us that the former has been found a much more certain road to the introduction of despotism than the latter, and that of those men who have overturned the liberties of republics, the greatest number have begun their career by paying an obsequious court to the people; commencing demagogues, and ending tyrants.

In the course of the preceding observations, I have had an eye, my fellow-citizens, to putting you upon your guard against all attempts, from whatever quarter, to influence your decision in a matter of the utmost moment to your welfare, by any impressions other than those which may result from the evidence of truth. You will, no doubt, at the same time, have collected from the general scope of them, that they proceed from a source not unfriendly to the new Constitution. Yes, my countrymen, I own to you that, after having given it an attentive consideration, I am clearly of opinion it is your interest to adopt it. I am convinced that this is the safest course for your liberty, your dignity, and your happiness. I affect not reserves which I do not feel. I will not amuse you with an appearance of deliberation when I have decided. I frankly acknowledge to you my convictions, and I will freely lay before you the reasons on which they are founded. The consciousness of good intentions disdains ambiguity. I shall not, however, multiply professions on this head. My motives must remain in the depository of my own breast. My arguments will be open to all, and may be judged of by all. They shall at least be offered in a spirit which will not disgrace the cause of truth.

I propose, in a series of papers, to discuss the following interesting particulars:

THE UTILITY OF THE UNION TO YOUR POLITICAL PROSPERITY THE INSUFFICIENCY OF THE PRESENT CONFEDERATION TO PRESERVE THAT UNION THE NECESSITY OF A GOVERNMENT AT LEAST EQUALLY ENERGETIC WITH THE ONE PROPOSED, TO THE ATTAINMENT OF THIS OBJECT THE CONFORMITY OF THE PROPOSED CONSTITUTION TO THE TRUE PRINCIPLES OF REPUBLICAN GOVERNMENT ITS ANALOGY TO YOUR OWN STATE CONSTITUTION and lastly, THE ADDITIONAL SECURITY WHICH ITS ADOPTION WILL AFFORD TO THE PRESERVATION OF THAT SPECIES OF GOVERNMENT, TO LIBERTY, AND TO PROPERTY.

In the progress of this discussion I shall endeavor to give a satisfactory answer to all the objections which shall have made their appearance, that may seem to have any claim to your attention.

It may perhaps be thought superfluous to offer arguments to prove the utility of the UNION, a point, no doubt, deeply engraved on the hearts of the great body of the people in every State, and one, which it may be imagined, has no adversaries. But the fact is, that we already hear it whispered in the private circles of those who oppose the new Constitution, that the thirteen States are of too great extent for any general system, and that we must of necessity resort to separate confederacies of distinct portions of the whole.[1] This doctrine will, in all probability, be gradually propagated, till it has votaries enough to countenance an open avowal of it. For nothing can be more evident, to those who are able to take an enlarged view of the subject, than the alternative of an adoption of the new Constitution or a dismemberment of the Union. It will therefore be of use to begin by examining the advantages of that Union, the certain evils, and the probable dangers, to which every State will be exposed from its dissolution. This shall accordingly constitute the subject of my next address.

PUBLIUS.

[1] The same idea, tracing the arguments to their consequences, is held out in several of the late publications against the new Constitution.

No. 10
James Madison

To the People of the State of New York:

AMONG the numerous advantages promised by a well constructed Union, none deserves to be more accurately developed than its tendency to break and control the violence of faction. The friend of popular governments never finds himself so much alarmed for their character and fate, as when he contemplates their propensity to this dangerous vice. He will not fail, therefore, to set a due value on any plan which, without violating the principles to which he is attached, provides a proper cure for it. The instability, injustice, and confusion introduced into the public councils, have, in truth, been the mortal diseases under which popular governments have everywhere perished; as they continue to be the favorite and fruitful topics from which the adversaries to liberty derive their most specious declamations. The valuable improvements made by the American constitutions on the popular models, both ancient and modern, cannot certainly be too much admired; but it would be an unwarrantable partiality, to contend that they have as effectually obviated the danger on this side, as was wished and expected. Complaints are everywhere heard from our most considerate and virtuous citizens, equally the friends of public and private faith, and of public and personal liberty, that our governments are too unstable, that the public good is disregarded in the conflicts of rival parties, and that measures are too often decided, not according to the rules of justice and the rights of the minor party, but by the superior force of an interested and overbearing majority. However anxiously we may wish that these complaints had no foundation, the evidence, of known facts will not permit us to deny that they are in some degree true. It will be found, indeed, on a candid review of our situation, that some of the distresses under which we labor have been erroneously charged on the operation of our governments; but it will be found, at the same time, that other causes will not alone account for many of our heaviest misfortunes; and, particularly, for that prevailing and increasing distrust of public engagements, and alarm for private rights, which are echoed from one end of the continent to the other. These must be chiefly, if not wholly, effects of the unsteadiness and injustice with which a factious spirit has tainted our public administrations.

By a faction, I understand a number of citizens, whether amounting to a majority or a minority of the whole, who are united and actuated by some common impulse of passion, or of interest, adverse to the rights of other citizens, or to the permanent and aggregate interests of the community.

There are two methods of curing the mischiefs of faction: the one, by removing its causes; the other, by controlling its effects.

There are again two methods of removing the causes of faction: the one, by destroying the liberty which is essential to its existence; the other, by giving to every citizen the same opinions, the same passions, and the same interests.

It could never be more truly said than of the first remedy, that it was worse than the disease. Liberty is to faction what air is to fire, an aliment without which it instantly expires. But it could not be less fully to abolish liberty, which is essential to political life, because it nourishes faction, than it would be to wish the annihilation of air, which is essential to animal life, because it imparts to fire its destructive agency.

The second expedient is as impracticable as the first would be unwise. As long as the reason of man continues fallible, and he is at liberty to exercise it, different opinions will be formed. As long as the connection subsists between his reason and his self-love, his opinions and his passions will have a reciprocal influence on each other; and the former will be objects to which the latter will attach themselves. The diversity in the faculties of men, from which the rights of property originate, is not less an insuperable obstacle to a uniformity of interests. The protection of these faculties is the first object of government. From the protection of different and unequal faculties of acquiring property, the possession of different degrees and kinds of property immediately results; and from the influence of these on the sentiments and views of the respective proprietors, ensues a division of the society into different interests and parties.

The latent causes of faction are thus sown in the nature of man; and we see them everywhere brought into different degrees of activity, according to the different circumstances of civil society. A zeal for different opinions concerning religion, concerning government, and many other points, as well of speculation as of practice; an attachment to different leaders ambitiously contending for preeminence and power; or to persons of other descriptions whose fortunes have been interesting to the human passions, have, in turn, divided mankind into parties, inflamed them with mutual animosity, and rendered them much more disposed to vex and oppress each other than to cooperate for their common good. So strong is this propensity of mankind to fall into mutual animosities, that where no substantial occasion presents itself, the most frivolous and fanciful distinctions have been sufficient to kindle their unfriendly passions and excite their most violent conflicts. But the most common and durable source of factions has been the various and unequal distribution of property. Those who hold and those who are without property have ever formed distinct interests in society. Those who are creditors, and those who are debtors, fall under a like discrimination. A landed interest, a manufacturing interest, a mercantile interest, a moneyed interest, with many lesser interests, grow up of necessity in civilized nations, and divide them into different classes, actuated by different sentiments and views. The regulation of these various and interfering interests forms the principal task of modern legislation, and involves the spirit of party and faction in the necessary and ordinary operations of the government.

No man is allowed to be a judge in his own cause, because his interest would certainly bias his judgment, and, not improbably, corrupt his integrity. With equal, nay with greater reason, a body of men are unfit to be both judges and parties at the same time; yet what are many of the most important acts of legislation, but so many judicial determinations, not indeed concerning the rights of single persons, but concerning the rights of large bodies of citizens? And what are the different classes of legislators but advocates and parties to the causes which they determine? Is a law proposed concerning private debts? It is a question to which the creditors are parties on one side and the debtors on the other. Justice ought to hold the balance between them. Yet the parties are, and must be, themselves the judges; and the most numerous party, or, in other words, the most powerful faction must be expected to prevail. Shall domestic manufactures be encouraged, and in what degree, by restrictions on foreign manufactures? are questions which would be differently decided by the landed and the manufacturing classes, and probably by neither with a sole regard to justice and the public good. The apportionment of taxes on the various descriptions of property is an act which seems to require the most exact impartiality; yet there is, perhaps, no legislative act in which greater opportunity and temptation are given to a predominant party to trample on the rules of justice. Every shilling with which they overburden the inferior number, is a shilling saved to their own pockets.

It is in vain to say that enlightened statesmen will be able to adjust these clashing interests, and render them all subservient to the public good. Enlightened statesmen will not always be at the helm. Nor, in many cases, can such an adjustment be made at all without taking into view indirect and remote considerations, which will rarely prevail over the immediate interest which one party may find in disregarding the rights of another or the good of the whole.

The inference to which we are brought is, that the **CAUSES** of faction cannot be removed, and that relief is only to be sought in the means of controlling its **EFFECTS**.

If a faction consists of less than a majority, relief is supplied by the republican principle, which enables the majority to defeat its sinister views by regular vote. It may clog the administration, it may convulse the society; but it will be unable to execute and mask its violence under the forms of the Constitution. When a majority is included in a faction, the form of popular government, on the other hand, enables it to sacrifice to its ruling passion or interest both the public good and the rights of other citizens. To secure the public good and private rights against the danger of such a faction, and at the same time to preserve the spirit and the form of popular government, is then the great object to which our inquiries are directed. Let me add that it is the great desideratum by which this form of government can be rescued from the opprobrium under which it has so long labored, and be recommended to the esteem and adoption of mankind.

By what means is this object attainable? Evidently by one of two only. Either the existence of the same passion or interest in a majority at the same time must be prevented, or the majority, having such coexistent passion or interest, must be rendered, by their number and local situation, unable to concert and carry into effect schemes of oppression. If the impulse and the opportunity be suffered to coincide, we well know that neither moral nor religious motives can be relied on as an adequate control. They are not found to be such on the injustice and violence of individuals, and lose their efficacy in proportion to the number combined together, that is, in proportion as their efficacy becomes needful.

From this view of the subject it may be concluded that a pure democracy, by which I mean a society consisting of a small number of citizens, who assemble and administer the government in person, can admit of no cure for the mischiefs of faction. A common passion or interest will, in almost every case, be felt by a majority of the whole; a communication and concert result from the form of government itself; and there is nothing to check the inducements to sacrifice the weaker party or an obnoxious individual. Hence it is that such democracies have ever been spectacles of turbulence and contention; have ever been found incompatible with personal security or the rights of property; and have in general been as short in their lives as they have been violent in their deaths. Theoretic politicians, who have patronized this species of government, have erroneously supposed that by reducing mankind to a perfect equality in their political rights, they would, at the same time, be perfectly equalized and assimilated in their possessions, their opinions, and their passions.

A republic, by which I mean a government in which the scheme of representation takes place, opens a different prospect, and promises the cure for which we are seeking. Let us examine the points in which it varies from pure democracy, and we shall comprehend both the nature of the cure and the efficacy which it must derive from the Union.

The two great points of difference between a democracy and a republic are: first, the delegation of the government, in the latter, to a small number of citizens elected by the rest; secondly, the greater number of citizens, and greater sphere of country, over which the latter may be extended.

The effect of the first difference is, on the one hand, to refine and enlarge the public views, by passing them through the medium of a chosen body of citizens, whose wisdom may best discern the true interest of their country, and whose patriotism and love of justice will be least likely to sacrifice it to temporary or partial considerations. Under such a regulation, it may well happen that the public voice, pronounced by the representatives of the people, will be more consonant to the public good than if pronounced by the people themselves, convened for the purpose. On the other hand, the effect may be inverted. Men of factious tempers, of local prejudices, or of sinister designs, may, by intrigue, by corruption, or by other means, first obtain the suffrages, and then betray the interests, of the people. The question resulting is, whether small or extensive republics are more favorable to the election of proper guardians of the public weal; and it is clearly decided in favor of the latter by two obvious considerations:

In the first place, it is to be remarked that, however small the republic may be, the representatives must be raised to a certain number, in order to guard against the cabals of a few; and that, however large it may be, they must be limited to a certain number, in order to guard against the confusion of a multitude. Hence, the number of representatives in the two cases not being in proportion to that of the two constituents, and being proportionally greater in the small republic, it follows that, if the proportion of fit characters be not less in the large than in the small republic, the former will present a greater option, and consequently a greater probability of a fit choice.

In the next place, as each representative will be chosen by a greater number of citizens in the large than in the small republic, it will be more difficult for unworthy candidates to practice with success the vicious arts by which elections are too often carried; and the suffrages of the people being more free, will be more likely to centre in men who possess the most attractive merit and the most diffusive and established characters.

It must be confessed that in this, as in most other cases, there is a mean, on both sides of which inconveniences will be found to lie. By enlarging too much the number of electors, you render the representatives too little acquainted with all their local circumstances and lesser interests; as by reducing it too much, you render him unduly attached to these, and too little fit to comprehend and pursue great and national objects. The federal Constitution forms a happy combination in this respect; the great and aggregate interests being referred to the national, the local and particular to the State legislatures.

The other point of difference is, the greater number of citizens and extent of territory which may be brought within the compass of republican than of democratic government; and it is this circumstance principally which renders factious combinations less to be dreaded in the former than in the latter. The smaller the society, the fewer probably will be the distinct parties and interests composing it; the fewer the distinct parties and interests, the more frequently will a majority be found of the same party; and the smaller the number of individuals composing a majority, and the smaller the compass within which they are placed, the more easily will they concert and execute their plans of oppression. Extend the sphere, and you take in a greater variety of parties and interests; you make it less probable that a majority of the whole will have a common motive to invade the rights of other citizens; or if such a common motive exists, it will be more difficult for all who feel it to discover their own strength, and to act in unison with each other. Besides other impediments, it may be remarked that, where there is a consciousness of unjust or dishonorable purposes, communication is always checked by distrust in proportion to the number whose concurrence is necessary.

Hence, it clearly appears, that the same advantage which a republic has over a democracy, in controlling the effects of faction, is enjoyed by a large over a small republic,—is enjoyed by the Union over the States composing it. Does the advantage consist in the substitution of representatives whose enlightened views and virtuous sentiments render them superior to local prejudices and schemes of injustice? It will not be denied that the representation of the Union will be most likely to possess these requisite endowments. Does it consist in the greater security afforded by a greater variety of parties, against the event of any one party being able to outnumber and oppress the rest? In an equal degree does the increased variety of parties comprised within the Union, increase this security. Does it, in fine, consist in the greater obstacles opposed to the concert and accomplishment of the secret wishes of an unjust and interested majority? Here, again, the extent of the Union gives it the most palpable advantage.

The influence of factious leaders may kindle a flame within their particular States, but will be unable to spread a general conflagration through the other States. A religious sect may degenerate into a political faction in a part of the Confederacy; but the variety of sects dispersed over the entire face of it must secure the national councils against any danger from that source. A rage for paper money, for an abolition of debts, for an equal division of property, or for any other improper or wicked project, will be less apt to pervade the whole body of the Union than a particular member of it; in the same proportion as such a malady is more likely to taint a particular county or district, than an entire State.

In the extent and proper structure of the Union, therefore, we behold a republican remedy for the diseases most incident to republican government. And according to the degree of pleasure and pride we feel in being republicans, ought to be our zeal in cherishing the spirit and supporting the character of Federalists.

PUBLIUS.

No. 51
James Madison

TO WHAT expedient, then, shall we finally resort, for maintaining in practice the necessary partition of power among the several departments, as laid down in the Constitution? The only answer that can be given is, that as all these exterior provisions are found to be inadequate, the defect must be supplied, by so contriving the interior structure of the government as that its several constituent parts may, by their mutual relations, be the means of keeping each other in their proper places. Without presuming to undertake a full development of this important idea, I will hazard a few general observations, which may perhaps place it in a clearer light, and enable us to form a more correct judgment of the principles and structure of the government planned by the convention.

In order to lay a due foundation for that separate and distinct exercise of the different powers of government, which to a certain extent is admitted on all hands to be essential to the preservation of liberty, it is evident that each department should have a will of its own; and consequently should be so constituted that the members of each should have as little agency as possible in the appointment of the members of the others. Were this principle rigorously adhered to, it would require that all the appointments for the supreme executive, legislative, and judiciary magistracies should be drawn from the same fountain of authority, the people, through channels having no communication whatever with one another. Perhaps such a plan of constructing the several departments would be less difficult in practice than it may in contemplation appear. Some difficulties, however, and some additional expense would attend the execution of it. Some deviations, therefore, from the principle must be admitted. In the constitution of the judiciary department in particular, it might be inexpedient to insist rigorously on the principle: first, because peculiar qualifications being essential in the members, the primary consideration ought to be to select that mode of choice which best secures these qualifications; secondly, because the permanent tenure by which the appointments are held in that department, must soon destroy all sense of dependence on the authority conferring them.

It is equally evident, that the members of each department should be as little dependent as possible on those of the others, for the emoluments annexed to their offices. Were the executive magistrate, or the judges, not independent of the legislature in this particular, their independence in every other would be merely nominal. But the great security against a gradual concentration of the several powers in the same department, consists in giving to those who administer each department the necessary constitutional means and personal motives to resist encroachments of the others. The provision for defense must in this, as in all other cases, be made commensurate to the danger of attack. Ambition must be made to counteract ambition. The interest of the man must be connected with the constitutional rights of the place. It may be a reflection on human nature, that such devices should be necessary to control the abuses of government. But what is government itself, but the greatest of all reflections on human nature? If men were angels, no government would be necessary. If angels were to govern men, neither external nor internal controls on government would be necessary. In framing a government which is to be administered by men over men, the great difficulty lies in this: you must first enable the government to control the governed; and in the next place oblige it to control itself.

A dependence on the people is, no doubt, the primary control on the government; but experience has taught mankind the necessity of auxiliary precautions. This policy of supplying, by opposite and rival interests, the defect of better motives, might be traced through the whole system of human affairs, private as well as public. We see it particularly displayed in all the subordinate distributions of power, where the constant aim is to divide and arrange the several offices in such a manner as that each may be a check on the other that the private interest of every individual may be a sentinel over the public rights. These inventions of prudence cannot be less requisite in the distribution of the supreme powers of the State. But it is not possible to give to each department an equal power of self-defense. In republican government, the legislative authority necessarily predominates. The remedy for this inconveniency is to divide the legislature into different branches; and to render them, by different modes of election and different principles of action, as little connected with each other as the nature of their common functions and their common dependence on the society will admit. It may even be necessary to guard against dangerous encroachments by still further precautions. As the weight of the legislative authority requires that it should be thus divided, the weakness of the executive may require, on the other hand, that it should be fortified.

An absolute negative on the legislature appears, at first view, to be the natural defense with which the executive magistrate should be armed. But perhaps it would be neither altogether safe nor alone sufficient. On ordinary occasions it might not be exerted with the requisite firmness, and on extraordinary occasions it might be perfidiously abused. May not this defect of an absolute negative be supplied by some qualified connection between this weaker department and the weaker branch of the stronger department, by which the latter may be led to support the constitutional rights of the former, without being too much detached from the rights of its own department? If the principles on which these observations are founded be just, as I persuade myself they are, and they be applied as a criterion to the several State constitutions, and to the federal Constitution it will be found that if the latter does not perfectly correspond with them, the former are infinitely less able to bear such a test.

There are, moreover, two considerations particularly applicable to the federal system of America, which place that system in a very interesting point of view. First. In a single republic, all the power surrendered by the people is submitted to the administration of a single government; and the usurpations are guarded against by a division of the government into distinct and separate departments. In the compound republic of America, the power surrendered by the people is first divided between two distinct governments, and then the portion allotted to each subdivided among distinct and separate departments. Hence a double security arises to the rights of the people. The different governments will control each other, at the same time that each will be controlled by itself. Second. It is of great importance in a republic not only to guard the society against the oppression of its rulers, but to guard one part of the society against the injustice of the other part. Different interests necessarily exist in different classes of citizens. If a majority be united by a common interest, the rights of the minority will be insecure.

There are but two methods of providing against this evil: the one by creating a will in the community independent of the majority that is, of the society itself; the other, by comprehending in the society so many separate descriptions of citizens as will render an unjust combination of a majority of the whole very improbable, if not impracticable. The first method prevails in all governments possessing an hereditary or self-appointed authority. This, at best, is but a precarious security; because a power independent of the society may as well espouse the unjust views of the major, as the rightful interests of the minor party, and may possibly be turned against both parties. The second method will be exemplified in the federal republic of the United States. Whilst all authority in it will be derived from and dependent on the society, the society itself will be broken into so many parts, interests, and classes of citizens, that the rights of individuals, or of the minority, will be in little danger from interested combinations of the majority.

In a free government the security for civil rights must be the same as that for religious rights. It consists in the one case in the multiplicity of interests, and in the other in the multiplicity of sects. The degree of security in both cases will depend on the number of interests and sects; and this may be presumed to depend on the extent of country and number of people comprehended under the same government. This view of the subject must particularly recommend a proper federal system to all the sincere and considerate friends of republican government, since it shows that in exact proportion as the territory of the Union may be formed into more circumscribed Confederacies, or States oppressive combinations of a majority will be facilitated: the best security, under the republican forms, for the rights of every class of citizens, will be diminished: and consequently the stability and independence of some member of the government, the only other security, must be proportionately increased. Justice is the end of government. It is the end of civil society. It ever has been and ever will be pursued until it be obtained, or until liberty be lost in the pursuit. In a society under the forms of which the stronger faction can readily unite and oppress the weaker, anarchy may as truly be said to reign as in a state of nature, where the weaker individual is not secured against the violence of the stronger; and as, in the latter state, even the stronger individuals are prompted, by the uncertainty of their condition, to submit to a government which may protect the weak as well as themselves; so, in the former state, will the more powerful factions or parties be gradually induced, by a like motive, to wish for a government which will protect all parties, the weaker as well as the more powerful.

It can be little doubted that if the State of Rhode Island was separated from the Confederacy and left to itself, the insecurity of rights under the popular form of government within such narrow limits would be displayed by such reiterated oppressions of factious majorities that some power altogether independent of the people would soon be called for by the voice of the very factions whose misrule had proved the necessity of it. In the extended republic of the United States, and among the great variety of interests, parties, and sects which it embraces, a coalition of a majority of the whole society could seldom take place on any other principles than those of justice and the general good; whilst there being thus less danger to a minor from the will of a major party, there must be less pretext, also, to provide for the security of the former, by introducing into the government a will not dependent on the latter, or, in other words, a will independent of the society itself. It is no less certain than it is important, notwithstanding the contrary opinions which have been entertained, that the larger the society, provided it lie within a practical sphere, the more duly capable it will be of self-government. And happily for the REPUBLICAN CAUSE, the practicable sphere may be carried to a very great extent, by a judicious modification and mixture of the FEDERAL PRINCIPLE.

PUBLIUS.

Speech at Chicago, Illinois, July 10, 1858

Abraham Lincoln

Judge Douglas made two points upon my recent speech at Springfield. He says they are to be the issues of this campaign. The first one of these points he bases upon the language in a speech which I delivered at Springfield, which I believe I can quote correctly from memory. I said there that "we are now far into the fifth year since a policy was instituted for the avowed object and with the confident promise of putting an end to slavery agitation; under the operation of that policy, that agitation had only not ceased, but has constantly augmented. I believe it will not cease until a crisis shall have been reached and passed. A house divided against itself cannot stand. I believe this government cannot endure permanently half slave and half free. I do not expect the Union to be dissolved," — I am quoting from my speech — "I do not expect the house to fall, but I do expect it will cease to be divided. It will become all one thing or the other. Either the opponents of slavery will arrest the spread of it, and place it where the public mind shall rest in the belief that it is in the course of ultimate extinction, or its advocates will push it forward until it shall become alike lawful in all the States, North as well as South."

In this paragraph ... Judge Douglas thinks he discovers great political heresy. I want your attention particularly to what he has inferred from it. He says I am in favor of making all the States of this Union uniform in all their internal regulations; that in all their domestic concerns I am in favor of making them entirely uniform. He draws this inference from the language I have quoted to you. He says that I am in favor of making war by the North upon the South for the extinction of slavery; that I am also in favor of inviting (as he expresses it) the South to a war upon the North, for the purpose of nationalizing slavery. Now, it is singular enough, if you will carefully read that passage over, that I did not say that I was in favor of anything in it. I only said what I expected would take place. I made a prediction only — it may have been a foolish one perhaps. I did not even say that I desired that slavery should be put in course of ultimate extinction. I do say so now, however, so there need be no longer any difficulty about that. It may be written down in the great speech.

Gentlemen, Judge Douglas informed you that this speech of mine was probably carefully prepared. I admit that it was. I am not master of language; I have not a fine education; I am not capable of entering into a disquisition upon dialectics, as I believe you call it; but I do not believe the language I employed bears any such construction as Judge Douglas put upon it. But I don't care about a quibble in regard to words. I know what I meant, and I will not leave this crowd in doubt, if I can explain it to them, what I really meant in the use of that paragraph.

I am not, in the first place, unaware that this Government has endured eighty-two years, half slave and half free. I know that. I am tolerably well acquainted with the history of the country, and I know that it has endured eighty-two years, half slave and half free. I believe — and that is what I meant to allude to there — I believe it has endured because, during all that time, until the introduction of the Nebraska Bill, the public mind did rest, all the time, in the belief that slavery was in course of ultimate extinction. That was what gave us the rest that we had through that period of eighty-two years; at least, so I believe. I have always hated slavery, I think as much as any Abolitionist. I have been an Old Line Whig. I have always hated it, but I have always been quiet about it until this new era of the introduction of the Nebraska Bill began. I always believed that everybody was against it, and that it was in course of ultimate extinction.... [T]he great mass of the nation have rested in the belief that slavery was in course of ultimate extinction. They had reason so to believe.

The adoption of the Constitution and its attendant history led the people to believe so; and that such was the belief of the framers of the Constitution itself. Why did those old men, about the time of the adoption of the Constitution, decree that Slavery should not go into the new territory, where it had not already gone? Why declare that within twenty years the African Slave Trade, by which slaves are supplied, might be cut off by Congress? Why were all these acts? I might enumerate more of these acts — but enough. What were they but a clear indication that the framers of the Constitution intended and expected the ultimate extinction of that institution. And now, when I say, as I said in my speech that Judge Douglas has quoted from, when I say that I think the opponents of slavery will resist the farther spread of it, and place it where the public mind shall rest with the belief that it is in course of ultimate extinction, I only mean to say, that they will place it where the founders of this Government originally placed it. ...

Now in relation to his inference that I am in favor of a general consolidation of all the local institutions of the various States. I will attend to that for a little while, and try to inquire, if I can, how on earth it could be that any man could draw such an inference from anything I said. I have said, very many times, in Judge Douglas' hearing, that no man believed more than I in the principle of self-government; that it lies at the bottom of all my ideas of just government, from beginning to end. I have denied that his use of that term applies properly. But for the thing itself, I deny that any man has ever gone ahead of me in his devotion to the principle, whatever he may have done in efficiency in advocating it. I think that I have said it in your hearing — that I believe each individual is naturally entitled to do as he pleases with himself and the fruit of his labor, so far as it in no wise interferes with any other man's rights — that each community, as a State, has a right to do exactly as it pleases with all the concerns within that State that interfere with the rights of no other State, and that the general government, upon principle, has no right to interfere with anything other than that general class of things that does concern the whole. I have said that at all times. I have said, as illustrations, that I do not believe in the right of Illinois to interfere with the cranberry laws of Indiana, the oyster laws of Virginia, or the Liquor Laws of Maine. I have said these things over and over again, and I repeat them here as my sentiments.

How is it, then, that Judge Douglas infers, because I hope to see slavery put where the public mind shall rest in the belief that it is in the course of ultimate extinction, that I am in favor of Illinois going over and interfering with the cranberry laws of Indiana? What can authorize him to draw any such inference? I suppose there might be one thing that at least enabled him to draw such an inference that would not be true with me or with many others, that is, because he looks upon all this matter of slavery as an exceedingly little thing — this matter of keeping one-sixth of the population of the whole nation in a state of oppression and tyranny unequalled in the world. He looks upon it as being an exceedingly little thing — only equal to the question of the cranberry laws of Indiana—as something having no moral question in it — as something on a par with the question of whether a man shall pasture his land with cattle, or plant it with tobacco — so little and so small a thing, that he concludes, if I could desire that anything should be done to bring about the ultimate extinction of that little thing, I must be in favor of bringing about an amalgamation of all the other little things in the Union. Now, it so happens — and there, I presume, is the foundation of this mistake — that the Judge thinks thus; and it so happens that there is a vast portion of the American people that do not look upon that matter as being this very little thing. They look upon it as a vast moral evil; they can prove it is such by the writings of those who gave us the blessings of liberty which we enjoy, and that they so looked upon it, and not as an evil merely confining itself to the States where it is situated; and while we agree that, by the Constitution we assented to, in the States where it exists we have no right to interfere with it because it is in the Constitution and we are by both duty and inclination to stick by that

Constitution in all its letter and spirit from beginning to end.

* * * * *

Now, it happens that we meet together once every year, sometime about the 4th of July, for some reason or other. These 4th of July gatherings I suppose have their uses. If you will indulge me, I will state what I suppose to be some of them.

We are now a mighty nation, we are thirty — or about thirty millions of people, and we own and inhabit about one-fifteenth part of the dry land of the whole earth. We run our memory back over the pages of history for about eighty-two years and we discover that we were then a very small people in point of numbers, vastly inferior to what we are now, with a vastly less extent of country, — with vastly less of everything we deem desirable among men, — we look upon the change as exceedingly advantageous to us and to our posterity, and we fix upon something that happened away back, as in some way or other being connected with this rise of prosperity. We find a race of men living in that day whom we claim as our fathers and grandfathers; they were iron men, they fought for the principle that they were contending for; and we understood that by what they then did it has followed that the degree of prosperity that we now enjoy has come to us. We hold this annual celebration to remind ourselves of all the good done in this process of time of how it was done and who did it, and how we are historically connected with it; and we go from these meetings in better humor with ourselves — we feel more attached the one to the other and more firmly bound to the country we inhabit. In every way we are better men in the age, and race, and country in which we live for these celebrations. But after we have done all this we have not yet reached the whole. There is something else connected with it. We have besides these men — descended by blood from our ancestors — among us perhaps half our people who are not descendants at all of these men, they are men who have come from Europe — German, Irish, French and Scandinavian — men that have come from Europe themselves, or whose ancestors have come hither and settled here, finding themselves our equals in all things. If they look back through this history to trace their connection with those days by blood, they find they have none, they cannot carry themselves back into that glorious epoch and make themselves feel that they are part of us, but when they look through that old Declaration of Independence they find that those old men say that "We hold these truths to be self-evident, that all men are created equal," and then they feel that that moral sentiment taught in that day evidences their relation to those men, that it is the father of all moral principle in them, and that they have a right to claim it as though they were blood of the blood, and flesh of the flesh of the men who wrote that Declaration, and so they are.

That is the electric cord in that Declaration that links the hearts of patriotic and liberty-loving men together, that will link those patriotic hearts as long as the love of freedom exists in the minds of men throughout the world.

Now, sirs, for the purpose of squaring things with this idea of "don't care if slavery is voted up or voted down," for sustaining the Dred Scott decision, for holding that the Declaration of Independence did not mean anything at all, we have Judge Douglas giving his exposition of what the Declaration of Independence means, and we have him saying that the people of America are equal to the people of England. According to his construction, you Germans are not connected with it. Now I ask you in all soberness, if all these things, if indulged in, if ratified, if confirmed and endorsed, if taught to our children, and repeated to them, do not tend to rub out the sentiment of liberty in the country, and to transform this Government into a government of some other form. Those arguments that are made, that the inferior race are to be treated with as much allowance as they are capable of enjoying; that as much is to be done for them as their condition will allow. What are these arguments? They are the arguments that kings have made for enslaving the people in all ages of the world. You will find that all the arguments in favor of king-craft were of this class; they always bestrode the necks of the people, not that they wanted to do it, but because the people were better off for being ridden. That is their argument, and this argument of the Judge is the same old serpent that says you work and I eat, you toil and I will enjoy the fruits of it. Turn in whatever way you will — whether it come from the mouth of a King, an excuse for enslaving the people of his country, or from the mouth of men of one race as a reason for enslaving the men of another race, it is all the same old serpent, and I hold if that course of argumentation that is made for the purpose of convincing the public mind that we should not care about this, should be granted, it does not stop with the negro. I should like to know if taking this old Declaration of Independence, which declares that all men are equal upon principle and making exceptions to it where will it stop. If one man says it does not mean a negro, why not another say it does not mean some other man? If that declaration is not the truth, let us get the Statute book, in which we find it and tear it out! Who is so bold as to do it! If it is not true let us tear it out! [Cries of "no, no."] Let us stick to it then, let us stand firmly by it then.

It may be argued that there are certain conditions that make necessities and impose them upon us, and to the extent that a necessity is imposed upon a man he must submit to it. I think that was the condition in which we found ourselves when we established this government. We had slavery among us, we could not get our constitution unless we permitted them to remain in slavery, we could not secure the good we did secure if we grasped for more, and having by necessity submitted to that much, it does not destroy the principle that is the charter of our liberties. Let that charter stand as our standard.

My friend has said to me that I am a poor hand to quote Scripture. I will try it again, however. It is said in one of the admonitions of the Lord, "As your Father in Heaven is perfect, be ye also perfect." The Savior, I suppose, did not expect that any human creature could be perfect as the Father in Heaven; but He said, "As your Father in Heaven is perfect, be ye also perfect." He set that up as a standard, and he who did most towards reaching that standard, attained the highest degree of moral perfection. So I say in relation to the principle that all men are created equal, let it be as nearly reached as we can. If we cannot give freedom to every creature, let us do nothing that will impose slavery upon any other creature. Let us then turn this government back into the channel in which the framers of the Constitution originally placed it. Let us stand firmly by each other. If we do not do so we are turning in the contrary direction, that our friend Judge Douglas proposes — not intentionally — as working in the traces tend to make this one universal slave nation. He is one that runs in that direction, and as such I resist him.

My friends, I have detained you about as long as I desired to do, and I have only to say, let us discard all this quibbling about this man and the other man — this race and that race and the other race being inferior, and therefore they must be placed in an inferior position — discarding our standard that we have left us. Let us discard all these things, and unite as one people throughout this land, until we shall once more stand up declaring that all men are created equal.

My friends, I could not, without launching off upon some new topic, which would detain you too long, continue to-night. I thank you for this most extensive audience that you have furnished me to-night. I leave you, hoping that the lamp of liberty will burn in your bosoms until there shall no longer be a doubt that all men are created free and equal.

About the Author

Photo by Anton Brkic

JOHN AGRESTO's academic career has spanned teaching at the University of Toronto, Kenyon College, Duke University, Wabash College, and the New School University. In the late 1970s he was both a scholar and administrator at the National Humanities Center in North Carolina, and in the 1980s he served in both senior administrative and policy positions the National Endowment for the Humanities. In 1989, he became President of St. John's College in Santa Fe, a position he served in for 11 years.

In 2003, Agresto went to Iraq, where he was the Senior Advisor for Higher Education and Scientific Research for the Coalition Provisional Authority. He returned regularly to Iraq over the years, becoming, in 2007, Acting Chancellor, Provost, and Academic Dean at the American University of Iraq in Sulaimani, positions he held until 2010. He was also, at various times, the Lilly Senior Research Fellow at Wabash College, Scholar-in-Residence at Hampden-Sidney College, and Fellow at the Madison Program in American Ideals and Institutions at Princeton University.

Widely published in the areas of politics, law, and education, Agresto is the author or editor of four books, including *Mugged by Reality: The Liberation of Iraq and the Failure of Good Intentions*; *The Supreme Court and Constitutional Democracy*; *The Humanist as Citizen: Essays on the Uses of the Humanities*; as well as *Tomatoes, Basil, and Olive Oil — An Italian American Cookbook*.

Though retired, Agresto remains President of John Agresto & Associates, an educational consulting company, and is also a member and former chair of the New Mexico State Advisory Committee to the U.S. Commission on Civil Rights.